IBN 'ABD AL-SALAM (D. 660)

THE BELIEF OF THE PEOPLE OF TRUTH

(AL-MULHA FÎ I'TIQÂD AHL AL-HAQQ)

Translation and Notes by
Gibril Fouad Haddad

Damascus
1998

بِسْمِ اللهِ الرَّحْمَنِ الرَّحِيمِ

وَصَلَّى اللهُ عَلَى سَيِّدِنَا مُحَمَّدٍ وَعَلَى آلِهِ وَصَحْبِهِ وَسَلَّمَ

رَبِّ يَسِّرْ وَلَا تُعَسِّرْ

This work is humbly dedicated to

Mawlana al-Shaykh Muhammad Nazim Adil al-Qubrusi al-Naqshbandi al-Haqqani,

to Shaykh Muhammad Hisham Kabbani
and their friends and followers worldwide,
and to Shaykh al-Sayyid Muhammad ibn Ibrahim al-Yaʿqubi,
at whose request this translation was undertaken.

"The *Mu'tazila* said: Allah's speech is created, invented, and brought into being. The *Hashwiyya*, who attribute a body to Allah, said: The alphabetical characters *(al-hurûf al-muqatta'a)*, the materials on which they are written, the colors in which they are written, and all that is between the two covers [of the volumes of Qur'an] is beginningless and preternal *(qadîma azaliyya)*. Al-Ash'ari took a middle road between them and said: The Qur'an is Allah's beginningless speech unchanged, uncreated, not of recent origin in time, nor brought into being. As for the alphabetical characters, the materials, the colors, the voices, the elements that are subject to limitations *(al-mahdûdât)*, and all that is subject to modality *(al-mukayyafât)* in the world: all this is created, originated, and produced." IBN 'ASAKIR, *TABYIN KADHIB AL-MUFTARI.*

"For one to say: 'I believe, in the matter of the Attributes, just what the *Salaf* believed' is a lie. How does he believe what he has no idea about, and the meaning of which he does not know?" IBN 'ABD AL-SALAM, *FATAWA.*

As-Sunna Foundation of America is an affiliate of the Islamic Supreme Council of America. The Islamiç Supreme Council of America is a non-profit, non-governmental organization dedicated to working for the cause of Islam on a bilateral level. As an affiliate of ISCA, ASFA strives to promote unity among Muslims and understanding and awareness about mainstream Islam through education. Its focus is on publishing works that support traditional, accepted approaches to Islamic jurisprudence and law.

ISBN: 95-930409-02-8

Published by:
As-Sunna Foundation of America
2415 Owen Rd Ste B
Fenton, MI 48430
email: asfa@sunnah.org

www.sunnah.org
www.islamicsupremecouncil.org

Foreword

Bismillahir-Rahmanir-Raheem

All praise is due to Allah Almighty who has revived in the hearts of His servants thirst for understanding the Islamic doctrine, *al-'aqeedah*. Blessings and salutations on His Beloved Servant Muhammad ﷺ, whom He raised to the station of nearness and whom he blessed with the revelation of Divine Guidance.

As-Sunna Foundation of America is honored to make available to the reading public this new set of translations of classical Islamic texts – the *Islamic Doctrines and Beliefs* series. We congratulate Dr. Gabriel Haddad for his efforts in bringing these outstanding classical manuscripts to light in the English language, as these books are a necessity for every Muslim home, school, library and university.

These works have reached us through distant centuries, authored by scholars who spent the whole of their lives in devotion to Allah and to spreading the knowledge of His great religion. They will undoubtedly stand witness for their authors on the Day of Judgment, wherein *"Whoever works righteousness benefits his own soul"* [41: 46], for every drop of blood running in the veins of such pious and sincere sages was infused with their intense devotion to preserve the fundamentals and the branches of Islam. Reliance on classical texts such as this one by 'Sultan al-'ulama Imam Al-'Izz ibn 'Abd as-Salam leaves little room for the introduction of alien creeds or uneducated speculation. Due to the extravagant efforts scholars made to compile these books, they are comprehensible and applicable to the general reader and student of religion.

Likewise the efforts of Dr. Haddad, who spent long days and nights in perfecting these translations, is something that we pray will be highly rewarded in this life and the next, for his intention and ours is to broadcast and clarify the pure and unadulterated teachings of *Ahl as-Sunna wal-Jama'a,* The People of the Sunnah and the Majority, whose foundations were laid by the Prophet ﷺ under the direction of his Lord, whose walls were erected by the *Salaf as-saliheen*, the pious predecessors, and whose roof and domes were built by the *Khalaf as-sadiqeen*, the truthful successors up to the present age.

The Importance of Knowledge of Correct *'Aqeedah*

Due to the fact that every generation witnesses a silent decline in worshippers' knowledge of the fundamental doctrines and beliefs of religion, constant efforts are required to elucidate and preserve the sources of this knowledge and to preserve them in the hearts and minds of Allah's servants. The acquisition of knowledge is obligatory for every accountable Muslim, for without it the appearance of conjecture and uneducated opinion is inevitable. Therein lies a danger that leads to an erroneous understanding of faith, which if left unchecked, may lead the seeker to a dangerous precipice from which he is unable to escape a serious fall.

The correct understanding of the signs of Allah Almighty, His Angels, His Books, His Prophets, the Day of Judgment, and the Divine Decree saves one from two extremes: denial of Allah's attributes, and its opposite anthropomorphism, the relating of Allah's attributes to physical manifestations.

There is no time better than today to introduce these books to those for whom English is the mother tongue, for the subject of *'aqeedah* has become one of controversy and confusion. These books provide a classical approach to understanding Islamic doctrine, based on some of the most accepted and reliable scholars of *Ahl as-Sunnah wal-Jama'ah,* the Saved Group.

Praise be to Allah, Lord of the Worlds, and salutations and blessings of peace on His Perfect Servant, Muhammad ﷺ.

Shaykh Muhammad Hisham Kabbani
1 Ramadan, 1420
December 8, 1999
Fenton, Michigan, USA

Contents

Ibn 'Abd Al-Salam (577-660)

The Belief of the People of Truth

Appendices

Bibliography 91

Ibn 'Abd Al-Salam (577-660)

'Izz al-Din Abu Muhammad 'Abd al-'Aziz ibn 'Abd al-Salam ibn Abi al-Qasim ibn Hasan ibn Muhammad ibn Muhadhdhab al-Sulami al-Dimashqi al-Shafi'i, named by al-Dhahabi "the Imam, erudite scholar, jurist, *mujtahid*, Proof of Islam, and *Shaykh of Islam*" known as *Sultan al-'Ulama'* as stated by Ibn al-Subki, Ibn 'Imad, and others. Born in Damascus, he studied under Fakhr al-Din al-Qasim ibn 'Asakir, Jamal al-Din ibn al-Harastani, al-Amidi and others until he acquired a thorough knowledge of the Shafi'i school, the principles of jurisprudence, and the Arabic language. He achieved the rank of *ijtihâd* and became the foremost Shafi'i authority in his time, known also for his great piety and devotion to worship. Among his students were the imams and hadith masters al-Dimyati, Ibn Daqiq al-'Id who named him *Sultan al-'Ulama'* and *Shaykh al-Islam*, Abu al-Husayn al-Yunini,[1] Abu Shama, and others. He taught in several schools and was the head preacher in Damascus then in Cairo where he sat as a judge.

Al-Dhahabi and Ibn al-Subki relate from Abu Shama that when Ibn 'Abd al-Salam assumed the post of head preacher in the Umawi mosque in Damascus he eliminated many of the innovations that had crept into the practice of the people:

- He eliminated the color black, the rhymed prose *(saj')*, and the donning of the *taylasân* by preachers.[2]

- He eliminated the triple striking of the sword on the ground by the preacher or the *mu'adhdhin* before the *khutba*.

- He ordered that only one person raise the *adhân* when he sat down before the first *khutba*.

- He left out praise of kings from the pulpit and replaced it with supplication to Allah.

---

[1]This is the imam and hadith master Sharaf al-Din Abu al-Husayn 'Ali ibn Shaykh al-Islam Muhammad ibn Ahmad al-Yunini al-Ba'labakki al-Hanbali (621-701), famous for his meticulous transmission of Bukhari's *Sahih*. Al-Dhahabi accompanied him and narrated from him in Ba'labak and Damascus, as related in the *Siyar A'lam al-Nubala'* (17:120 #6086).

[2]The *taylasân* is a kind of unstitched, unhemmed cloth worn on the head or the shoulders. Bukhari narrated from Anas ibn Malik that the latter looked at the *Jum'a* congregation and, seeing a *taylasân*, said: "They look just like the Jews of Khaybar!"

- He instructed all mosques not to raise the *iqâma* directly after the *adhân* of sunset, but to wait a few moments.[3]

- He replaced the non-Sunna recitation of the verse ❴**Lo! Allah and His angels shower blessings on the Prophet**❵ (33:56) after congregational prayers with the Sunna recitation of the invocation: "There is no God except Allah, His is the dominion, His is the praise, and He is able to do all things."[4]

- He declared invalid in 637 the practice of congregational prayer for the nights of mid-Sha'ban *(salât nisf sha'bân)* and the twelve *rak'as* prayed in the first *Jum'a* of Rajab *(salât al-raghâ'ib)*.

The hadith master Ibn al-Salah responded to the latter *fatwâ* by a contrary *fatwâ*, whereupon Ibn 'Abd al-Salam published an epistle entitled *al-Targhib 'an Salat al-Ragha'ib al-Mawdu'a wa Bayan Ma Fiha Min Mukhalafa al-Sunan al-Mashru'a* ("The Dissuasion From the Fabricated *Salat al-Ragha'ib* and Exposition of Its Contraventions of the Prophet's 鬱 Instituted Sunnas"). Ibn al-Salah responded by publishing a refutation, which Ibn 'Abd al-Salam followed up with a counter-refutation.[5] Ibn al-Salah's argument was that such prayers cannot be prohibited merely because the hadith adduced for them is weak, as their practice is supported by the general command to pray in the Book and the Sunna. Ibn 'Abd al-Salam's argument was more precise in that *salat al-ragha'ib* is in direct contradiction of specific hadiths of the Prophet's 鬱 such as:

- The encouragement to pray supererogatory prayers – other than the specific occasions of the Two Feasts, *Tarawih*, eclipses, and great needs such as supplication for rain – alone and in one's house.[6]

---

[3]So as to allow time for the two *rak'as* of *sunna* before *maghrib*, which are desirable *(mustahabba)* according to the correct position of the Shafi'i school as stated by al-Nawawi in *Sharh Sahih Muslim*. See al-'Iraqi, *Tarh al-Tathrib* (3:33).

[4]Hadith of the Prophet 鬱 which he uttered and ordered congregations to utter after every prayer as narrated from several Companions by Bukhari, Muslim, al-Tirmidhi, Abu Dawud, and others.

[5]These texts were published under the title *Musajala 'Ilmiyya Bayn al-Imamayn al-Jalilayn al-'Izz ibn 'Abd al-Salam wa Ibn al-Salah*, eds. Muhammad Nasir al-Din al-Albani and Zuhayr al-Shawish (Beirut: al-Maktab al-Islami, 1961 and 1985).

[6]In Bukhari and Muslim: "The best prayer after the prescribed prayers is that prayed alone in one's house."

- The prohibition from singling out the night of *Jum'a* for supere-rogatory prayers and its day for fasting.[7]

At any rate, the fact that there exists disagreement among the scholars about any practice in Islam is enough cause to preclude prohibition of that practice. Al-Nawawi explicitly stated: "Scholars only protest against that which musters unanimous consensus; as for what does not muster unanimous consensus, then there is no [permission to] protest, as every *mujtahid* is correct according to one of the two views on the issue."[8] This is reiterated verbatim by Ibn Taymiyya.[9]

Ibn 'Abd al-Salam was gentle and good-natured, but fearless in telling the truth to kings even at the risk of his own life. When al-Malik al-Salih Isma'il took control of Damascus and gave away al-Shaqif and Safad to the Franks in 640, Ibn 'Abd al-Salam stopped praying for him from the pulpit, for which he was imprisoned then exiled together with Ibn al-Hajib al-Maliki. He went to Egypt where the Sultan al-Malik Mu'in al-Din Ayub ibn al-Kamil received him, and remained there until his death twenty years later. He taught in the Salihiyya school, sat as the chief judge of Egypt, and preached in the great Cairo mosque. The "mountain of hadith mastership" *(al-hâfiz al-jabal)* in Egypt, Zaki al-Din al-Mundhiri said: "We used to give *fatwâ* before Shaykh 'Izz al-Din came. After he came, giving *fatwâ* was restricted to him."[10]

Taqi al-Din al-Subki narrated from his shaykh ['Ali ibn Muhammad ibn Khattab, 'Ala' al-Din Abu al-Hasan] al-Baji:

> Our shaykh 'Izz al-Din went up to the Sultan's castle one time, on the day of *'Id*. He saw the army in full array before the Sultan's court and the Sultan's splendor for the occasion according to the custom in the lands of Egypt, with the princes and leaders kissing the ground in front of him. The Shaykh turned to the Sultan and called out to him, saying: "O Ayyub! What will your argument be when Allah tells you: Did I

---

[7]Narrated from Abu Hurayra by Muslim.

[8]Al-Nawawi, *Sharh Sahih Muslim*, Chapter entitled *Al-Amr bi al-Ma'ruf wa al-Nahy 'an al-Munkar*, hadith of the Prophet 鐵: "Whoever of you sees wrongdoing, let him change it with his hand; if he cannot, then with his tongue; if he cannot, then with his heart, and that is the weakest belief." Narrated from Sa'id al-Khudri by Muslim.

[9]In *al-Fatawa al-Kubra* (Dar al-ma'rifa ed. 2:33).

[10]Ibn al-Subki, *Tabaqat al-Shafi'iyya al-Kubra* (8:211).

not give you the kingdom of Egypt, and then you permitted wine?" The Sultan said: "Is this the case?" The shaykh said: "Yes! Wine is sold in such-and-such a tavern" – he mentioned other wrong-doings – "while you are basking in the luxury of this kingdom!" He was shouting at the top of his voice in front of the entire army. The Sultan said: "My master, I am not the one who did this. This is from the time of my father." The Shaykh replied: "So you are of those who say: ❴**Lo! we found our fathers following a religion, and we are guided by their footprints**❵ (43:22)!" After this the Sultan gave an edict to shut down the tavern.... Later, I asked him: "Did you not fear addressing the Sultan in this manner?" He replied: "By Allah! My son, I recalled Allah's majesty in my heart, and the Sultan became like a kitten in front of me."[11]

He later resigned from all these posts after he learnt that the Sultan had disapproved of his destroying a tavern which had been built by some of his relatives on top of a mosque. He then isolated himself from public life and taught in his house.

Ibn 'Abd al-Salam lived through the dark days of the Mongol and Frankish onslaughts against the Muslims of al-Sham. He composed an epistle defining jihad and listing its duties and merits, and in his *Mulha fi I'tiqad Ahl al-Haqq* – translated in the present volume – refers to the obligation of the ruler of the Muslims never to relinquish armed struggle against the enemies of Islam:

> Allah has ordered us to struggle in the cause of His Religion. The only difference is that the scholar's weapons are his knowledge and his tongue, while the king's weapons are his swords and spears. Just as it is not allowed for kings to put down their weapons in the face of atheists and Christians, similarly, it is not allowed for scholars to still their tongues in the face of heretics and innovators.

---

[11]*Ibid.* (8:211-212).

His Defeat of the Anthropomorphists

Ibn 'Abd al-Salam's son Sharaf al-Din 'Abd al-Latif related that his father wrote *al-Mulha fi I'tiqad Ahl al-Haqq* in Damascus at the request of al-Malik al-Ashraf Musa ibn al-Malik al-'Adil ibn Ayyub, in refutation of certain heresies propagated by some Hanbalis on the anthropomorphist understanding of the "letter" of Qur'anic writing and the "voice" of Qur'anic recitation. Envious of the Sultan's love for Ibn 'Abd al-Salam, they had approached the Sultan with the following charges against Ibn 'Abd al-Salam:

> He is Ash'ari in his doctrine, he declares incorrect whoever believes [in the preternality of] the letter and voice of the Qur'an and declares them innovators, and part of his doctrine is that he affirms what al-Ash'ari said, namely, that bread does not sate, nor water quench thirst, nor fire burn.

The Sultan expressed doubt that this was Ibn 'Abd al-Salam's position, whereupon the Hanbalis issued a *fatwâ* on the preternality of the letter and the voice, challenging him to refute it. When news of this reached him, Ibn 'Abd al-Salam said: "This *fatwâ* is a test for me, and – by Allah! – I shall not respond except with the truth." Then he wrote *al-Mulha*.[12] The Hanbalis then took the *Mulha* to the Sultan in triumph, expecting to have Ibn 'Abd al-Salam executed on its basis. The Sultan expressed outrage at Ibn 'Abd al-Salam's position, and the only scholar to rise to his defense was Jamal al-Din Abu 'Amr ibn al-Hajib al-Maliki. The latter accused the ulama of remaining silent when they should have spoken out, and of suggesting to the Sultan that Ibn 'Abd al-Salam was wrong and his accusers right. He then convinced them to co-sign a *fatwâ* in support of Ibn 'Abd al-Salam's position.

Ibn 'Abd al-Salam then asked for a general meeting of the scholars of all Four Schools before the Sultan, but the latter sent him a stern letter of refusal in which he accused him of claiming independent *ijtihâd* and wanting to form a fifth School of Law. Ibn 'Abd al-Salam replied:

> The *fatwâ* issued [by us] on this question is agreed upon by the scholars of Islam – Shafi'is, Malikis, Hanafis, and the eminent ones of

---

[12]*Ibid.* (8:218).

7

the Hanbalis. None contradicts it except the riffraff about whom Allah ﷻ cares not a whit. This is the truth and it is impermissible to reject it, the correct position which can never be obviated. If the scholars convene before the Sultan's court, the Sultan will know the truth of what I say, and the Sultan is the most qualified of people to implement this. Those who kept silent did so at first, because of what they saw of the Sultan's anger. If they had not seen such anger they would not have given *fatwâ* in the beginning other than what their position is now. Nevertheless: Write what I said in my *fatwâ* and what the others said, then send it to the countries of Islam, so that every authority who must be followed can write about it and be relied upon in his own *fatwâ* concerning it; as for us we shall adduce the books of the authoritative scholars, so that the Sultan can see them for himself.... As for the mention of *ijtihâd* and the fifth School: there are no schools in the tenets of faith. The foundation is one, while differences are in the branches. The like of that talk comes from those upon whom you have relied in something for which it is impermissible to rely upon them. Allah knows best whoever knows his religion and stop at his limits. In conclusion we say that we are in Allah's party, and we are His helpers and soldiers, and a soldier that does not risk his life is not a soldier.

When the Sultan received the above reply he declared Ibn 'Abd al-Salam forbidden from giving *fatwâ*, confined to his house, and forbidden from meeting anyone. The latter said: "These stipulations are from Allah's great bounty for me."[13] Three days later, Shaykh Jamal al-Din al-Hasiri al-Hanafi visited the Sultan and convinced him that Ibn 'Abd al-Salam's words in the *Mulha* and his subsequent reply were "the doctrine of the Muslims, the rallying-cry of the pious, and the certitude of the believers," adding: "All that is in there is correct, and whoever contravenes it and goes to the beliefs of the opponents concerning the affirmation of the letter and the voice – he is a donkey." After this the Sultan expressed remorse and swore that he would make Ibn 'Abd al-Salam the wealthiest of scholars, returning him to his previous position of *fatwâ* and ordering that his books be read, and so until the Sultan's death.[14]

---

[13] *Ibid.* (8:232-235).
[14] *Ibid.* (8:236-237).

His Ash'arism

In the matter of the Names and Attributes Ibn 'Abd al-Salam was fundamentally an Ash'ari, as illustrated by his work on the principles of metaphorical interpretation of the Holy Qur'an entitled *Al-Ishara ila al-Ijaz fi Ba'd Anwa' al-Majaz*:

When Allah is described by something which is inapplicable to Him literally *(bî haqîqatihi)*, He is described by it only metaphorically…. As in the case of the following:

1. Mercy *(al-rahma)* = According to the Shaykh [al-Ash'ari], it means Allah's willing *(irâda)*, for His servant, whatever one that shows mercy wills for the one who is shown mercy.

2. Friendship *(al-mahabba)* = It entails willing munificence *(ikrâm)* towards the beloved and making him content *(irdâ')*.

3. Love *(al-wudd)* = Allah's will or treatment of the one He loves in the manner of the lover towards the beloved.

4. Contentment *(al-ridâ)* = Allah's will or treatment in the manner of the one who is content towards the one who made him content; in this sense it is an attribute of the Entity. Or, Allah's actual treatment in the manner of the one who is content towards the one who made him content; in this sense it is an attribute of act as in the hadith. Literally, it means peace of mind at whatever the mind is content with – and Allah is exalted above that.

5. Gratitude *(al-shukr)* = A metaphor based on similitude *(majâz al-tashbîh)* between His treatment towards one who obeys Him and the treatment of the grateful one towards one he thanks. Or a metonymy *(majâz tasmiya)* naming the result by the name of the cause, as to thank Him is expressed by obeying Him.[a]

---

[a] Abu Sahl al-Su'luki narrates that as a boy al-Junayd heard his uncle being asked about thankfulness, whereupon he said: "It is to not use His favors for the purpose of disobeying Him." In al-Qushayri, *Risala* (p. 148-150); Ibn 'Imad, *Shadharat al-Dhahab* (2:228-230); al-Dhahabi, *Siyar* (11:153-155 #2555); Ibn al-Subki, *Tabaqat* (2:260-275 #60).

6. Laughter *(al-dahik)* = His satisfaction *(ridâ)* and acceptance *(qabûl)*.

7. Happiness *(al-farah)* = He wills, for repentent sinners, whatever happiness brings about in the one who is happy. Or He treats the repentent sinners in the same manner as happiness treats the one who is happy.

8. Patience *(al-sabr)* = He treats His servants in the way that the patient one behaves towards what he dislikes. This is a metaphor based on similitude.

9. Jealousy *(al-ghîra)* = A metaphor of similitude with the legal category of abomination *(karâhiyya)* which applies to indecencies, or a metaphor for the emphatic repetition of the prohibition of indecencies.

10. Shyness or shame *(al-hayâ')* = A synechdoche *(majâz al-mulâzama)* naming as shame the abandonment of what causes shame. Or a metonymy *(majâz tasmiya)* naming that result by the name of the cause. Allah does not depart from right unlike one who shies from it.

11. His testing *(ibtilâ')* through benefits and wrongs, good and evil = A metaphor of similitude between Him and an examiner, although He knows everything.

12. His sarcasm *(sukhriyya)*, mockery *(istihza')*, scheming *(makr)*, and deceit *(khid')* = All of these are metaphors of similitude or metonymies naming the result by the name of its cause, His sarcasm being caused by theirs, His mockery by theirs, His scheming by theirs, and His deceit by theirs.

13. His astonishment *('ajab)* = A metaphor of similitude with either the ugliness of what causes astonishment or its excellence.

14. Reference to Him with the pronoun "That One" *(dhâlika, dhâlikum)* which indicates distance = The remoteness of His Entity from similitude with all other entities *(dhawât)*, and the remoteness of His Attributes from similitude with all other attributes.

15. His hesitancy *(taraddud)* = In the divine hadith "Nor do I hesitate to do anything as I hesitate to take back the believer's soul, for he hates death and I hate to hurt him,"[b] a metaphor of the superlative rank of the believer in Allah's presence and synechdoche for a lesser hurt to prevent a greater harm, as in the case of a father's severance of his son's gangrened hand so as to save his life.

16. His establishment *(istiwâ')* over the Throne = A metaphor for establishing dominion *(istilâ')* over His kingdom and disposing of it, as the poet said:

> *qad istawâ Bishrun 'ala al-'Irâq*
> *min ghayri sayfin wa damin muhrâq*
>
> *Bishr established mastery over Iraq*
> *without sword and without shedding blood.*[c]

It is a metaphor of similitude with kings, who dispose of the affairs of their kingdoms while sitting among the dynastic princes. The throne may also express rank, as in 'Umar's ⬡ saying: "My throne would have toppled if I had not found a merciful Lord."[d]

17. His freeing Himself in the verse {**We shall soon be free to dispose of you**} (55:31) = A metaphor of similitude for the immense significance attributed to the judgment of creatures.

18. The baring of His shin = A metaphor for His aggravation of the judgment of His enemies and their humiliation, defeat, and punishment. The Arabs say of one that acts earnestly and intensely that "he has bared his shin."

---

[b] *Hadith qudsi* of the Prophet ⬡ narrated from Abu Hurayra by Bukhari.

[c] See Appendix entitled "*Istiwâ'* is a Divine Act" in our translation of al-Bayhaqi's *al-Asma'*.

[d] Narrated as a dream seen after 'Umar's death, see the following under the entry *'arsh*: *Lisan al-'Arab*, Ibn al-Athir's *al-Nihaya*, al-Raghib's *Mufradat Alfaz al-Qur'an*, *al-Basa'ir* (4:24), and *'Umda al-Huffaz*.

19. His wrath *(ghadab)* = A metaphor of similitude for the attribute of act which consists in the punishment He exacts from those who disobey Him.

20. His resentment *(sukht or sakhat)* = Allah's will of whatever one who resents wills for the object of his resentment; or a metaphor of similitude; or a metonymy attributing resentment to their disbelief in the sense of attributing a verb to its cause.

21. His grief *(asaf)* = His anger. ❴**When they grieved Us, We exacted retribution from them**❵ (43:55) meaning "When they made us angry, we punished them."

22. His hatred *(qilâ)*: ❴**Your Lord has not forsaken you nor does He hate you**❵ (93:3) meaning "He has never forsaken you since He brought you near, nor hated you since He loved you."

23. His spite *(maqt)* i.e. the paroxysm of hatred *(bughd)* = Allah wills for the misguided whatever one who bears hatred wills for the object of his hate, or He curses or treats them in the manner that one who bears hatred curses or treats the object of his hate. Or it is a metaphor of similitude in terms of the above.

24. His enmity *('adâwa)* = His treatment of His enemies in a way so as to cause them harm for the most part.

25. His malediction *(la'n)* = His banishment of sinners from His door, far from His reward.[e]

---

[e] Ibn 'Abd al-Salam, *al-Ishara ila al-Ijaz* (p. 104-112).

His Tasawwuf

Ibn ʿAbd al-Salam deeply respected *tasawwuf* which he took from the Shafiʿi Shaykh al-Islam and Sufi master Shihab al-Din al-Suhrawardi (539-632), al-Dhahabi's grandshaykh, whom the latter calls: "The shaykh, the imam, the man of knowledge, the ascetic, the Knower of Allah, the hadith scholar, Shaykh al-Islam, the Peerless One of the Sufis... the Shaykh of his time in the science of Reality *('ilm al-haqîqa)*."[15] He also studied under the master and Spiritual Pole *(qutb)* Abu al-Hasan al-Shadhili (d. 656) and his disciple al-Mursi. The author of *Miftah al-Saʿada* and al-Subki in his *Tabaqat* relate that al-ʿIzz would say, upon hearing al-Shadhili and al-Mursi speaking: "This is a kind of speech that is fresh from Allah."[16] Ibn ʿImad al-Hanbali also relates from Ibn Shuhba that Ibn ʿAbd al-Salam had the gift of spiritual unveilings *(mukâshafât)*.[17]

In his two-volume *Qawaʿid al-Ahkam* on *usûl al-fiqh* he mentions that the Sufis are those meant by Allah's saying: ❨**Allah's party**❩ (5:56, 58:22), defining *tasawwuf* as "the betterment of hearts, through whose health bodies are healthy, and through whose disease bodies are diseased." He considers the knowledge of external legal rulings a knowledge of the Law in its generalities, while the knowledge of internal matters is a knowledge of the Law in its subtle details.[18]

In view of his strictness in every matter, he is famous for participating in *samâʿ* or recitals of spiritual poetry, and permitting the swaying of the body and "dancing" *(raqs)* associated with trances and other states of ecstasy during *samâʿ* and *dhikr*. It is authentically reported that he himself "attended the *samâʿ* and danced in states of ecstasy" *(kâna yahduru al-samâʿ wa yarqusu wa yatawâjad)*.[19] Part of the evidence adduced to

---

[15]Al-Dhahabi in the same chapter says: "My shaykh, the hadith scholar and ascetic Diya' al-din 'Isa ibn Yahya al-Ansari conferred upon me the cloak *(khirqa)* of *tasawwuf* in Cairo and said: 'Shaykh Shihab al-Din al-Suhrawardi conferred it upon me in Mecca from his uncle Abu al-Najib.'" Al-Dhahabi, *Siyar* (16:300-302 #5655). Like Ibn al-Jawzi, al-Suhrawardi is a descendent of Abu Bakr al-Siddiq ﷺ.

[16]*Miftah al-Saʿada* (2:353); al-Subki, *Tabaqat al-Shafiʿiyya al-Kubra* (8:214).

[17]In *Shadharat al-Dhahab* (5:302).

[18]Ibn ʿAbd al-Salam, *Qawaʿid al-Ahkam* (1:29, 2:212).

[19]Al-Dhahabi, *Siyar* (17:33); Ibn al-Subki, *Tabaqat al-Shafiʿiyya al-Kubra*; Ibn al-ʿImad, *Shadharat al-dhahab* (5:302); Ibn Shakir al-Kutabi, *Fawat al-Wafayat*

support the permissibility of this is the following authentic narration of 'Ali ibn Abi Talib :

> I visited the Prophet ﷺ with Ja'far [ibn Abi Talib] and Zayd [ibn Haritha]. The Prophet ﷺ said to Zayd: "You are my freedman" *(mawlây)*, whereupon Zayd began to hop on one leg around the Prophet *(hajila)*. The Prophet ﷺ then said to Ja'far: "You resemble me in my form and manners" *(khalqî wa khuluqî)*, whereupon Ja'far began to hop behind Zayd. The Prophet ﷺ then said to me: "You are part of me and I am part of you" *(anta minnî wa anâ mink)* whereupon I began to hop behind Ja'far.[20]

Some scholars have seen in this report evidence for the permissibility of dancing *(al-raqs)* upon hearing a recital that uplifts the spirit.[21] This qualified permissibility of dancing precludes the prohibition of *samâ'* or the *hadra* and that of the swaying that accompanies them. Imam Habib al-Haddad (d. 1995) addressed this issue in the following terms in his book *Miftah al-Janna*:

> *Dhikr* returns from the outward feature which is the tongue to the inward which is the heart, where it becomes solidly rooted, so that it takes firm hold of its members. The sweetness of this is tasted by the one who has taken to *dhikr* with the whole of himself, so that his skin and heart are softened. As Allah said: ❴**Then their skins and their hearts soften to the remembrance of Allah**❵" (39:23).

> The "softening of the heart" consists in the sensitivity and timidity that occur as a result of nearness and *tajallî* (manifestation). Sufficient is it to have Allah as one's intimate companion!

(1:595); al-Nabahani, *Jami' Karamat al-Awliya* (2:71); Abu al-Sa'adat, *Taj al-Ma'arif* (p. 250).

[20]Narrated from 'Ali by Ahmad in his *Musnad* with a sound chain as stated by Shakir (1:537 #857) and by al-Bazzar in his *Musnad* with a sound chain according to al-Haythami in *Majma' al-Zawa'id* (5:176). Ahmad's chain is graded as "strong" by al-Arna'ut in *Sahih Ibn Hibban* (15:520 #7046). Also narrated by al-Bayhaqi in *al-Sunan al-Kubra* (8:6 #15548, 10:226 #20816), Ibn Abi Shayba in his *Musannaf* (12:105), and Ibn Sa'd *mursal* in his *Tabaqat* (4[1]:22), chapter of Ja'far ibn Abi Talib.

[21]Al-Haytami, *Fatawa Hadithiyya* (p. 212); Al-Yafi'i, *Mir'at al-Jinan* (4:154). *Samâ'* is extensively defined in al-Qushayri's *Rasa'il*, al-Sarraj's *al-Luma'*, and al-Ghazali.

As for the "softening of the skin" this is the ecstasy and swaying from side to side which result from intimacy and manifestation, or from fear and awe. No blame is attached to someone who has reached this rank if he sways and chants, for in the painful throes of love and passion he finds something which arouses the highest yearning....

The exhortation provided by fear and awe brings forth tears and forces one to tremble and be humble. These are the states of the righteous believers *(abrâr)* when they hear the Speech and *dhikr* of Allah the Exalted. ❴**Their skins shiver**❵ (39:23), and then soften with their hearts and incline to *dhikr* of Him, as they are covered in serenity and dignity, so that they are neither frivolous, pretentious, noisy, or ostentatious. Allah the Exalted has not described them as people whose sense of reason has departed, who faint, dance, or jump about.[22]

As for the case where dancing is strictly prohibited, it regards the worldly kind of effeminate dancing which had little or nothing to do with the ecstasy of *samâ'* and *dhikr*. Ibn 'Abd al-Salam differentiated between the two:

Dancing is an innovation which is not countenanced except by one deficient in his mind. It is unfitting for other than women. As for the audition of poetry *(samâ')* which stirs one towards states of purity *(ahwâl saniyya)* which remind one of the hereafter: there is nothing wrong with it, nay, it is recommended *(yundab ilayh)* for lukewarm and dry hearts. However, the one who harbors wrong desires in his heart is not allowed to attend the *samâ'*, for it stirs up whatever desire is already in the heart, both the detestable and the desirable.[23]

It is in the above perspective that Imam Ibn Khafif said in *al-'Aqida al-Sahiha*:

119. Spiritual recital *(al-samâ')* is permissible for the knower, but null and void for the seeker.

---

[22]Al-Sayyid Habib Mashhur al-Haddad, *Key to the Garden*, trans. Mostafa Badawi (London: Quilliam Press, 1989 p. 116).
[23]Ibn 'Abd al-Salam, *Fatawa Misriyya* (p. 158).

120. Spiritual recital is neither a state nor an act of drawing near to Allah. It is better to leave it altogether because of its many evils and great dangers.[24]

Ibn 'Abd al-Salam also said in his *Qawa'id al-Ahkam*:

Dancing and clapping are a bad display resembling the display of women, which no one indulges except frivolous men or affected liars... whoever apprehends the greatness of Allah, it cannot be imagined that he will start dancing and clapping as these are not performed except by the crassly ignorant, not those who have merit and intelligence, and the proof of their ignorance is that the *Shari'a* has not cited any evidence for their action in the Qur'an and the Sunna, and none of the Prophets or their notable followers ever did it.[25]

Asked about al-Qushayri's and al-Ghazali's saying that the highest level among Allah's servants after Messengers and Prophets was that of saints *(awliya')*, then that of the scholars *('ulamâ')*, he replied:

Concerning the priority of the knowers of Allah over the knowers of Allah's rulings, the saying of the teacher Abu Hamid [al-Ghazali] is agreed upon. No reasonable person doubts that the knowers of Allah... are not only better than the knowers of Allah's rulings, but also better than those of the branches and the roots of the Religion, because the rank of a science is according to its immediate object.... Most of the time scholars are veiled from their knowledge of Allah and His attributes, otherwise they would be among the knowers of Allah whose knowledge is continuous, as befits the demand of true virtue. And how could the gnostics and the jurists be the same, when Allah says: ❨The noblest among you in Allah's sight are the most godwary❩ (49:13)?... By the "erudite" in His saying ❨The erudite among His bondsmen fear Allah alone❩ (35:28), He means those who know Him, His attributes, and His actions, not those who know His rulings.... A sign of the superiority of the knowers of Allah over the jurists is that Allah effects miracles at the hands of the former, but

---

[24]In Shatta, *Sira al-Shaykh Ibn Khafif* (p. 350).
[25]Ibn 'Abd al-Salam, *Qawa'id al-Ahkam* (2:186, 220-221).

never at the hands of the latter, except when they enter the path of the knowers and acquire their characteristics.[26]

Among Ibn 'Abd al-Salam's works:

- A condensed commentary of the Holy Qur'an
- An abridgment of Imam al-Haramayn's *al-Nihaya* entitled *al-Jam' Bayn al-Hawi wa al-Nihaya*
- *Mukhtasar Sahih Muslim.*
- *Qawa'id al-Ahkam fi Masalih al-Anam* ("The Foundations of Legal Rulings for the Benefit of Creatures")
- *Al-Imam fi Adilla al-Ahkam* ("The Leading Book Concerning the Proof-Texts of Legal Rulings")
- *Bidaya al-Sul fi Tafdil al-Rasul* ("The Beginning of the Quest Concerning the Superexcellence of the Prophet ﷺ")
- *al-Qawa'id al-Sughra*, a shorter version of the preceding, in which he states that the angels do not see their Lord.
- *Al-Amali* ("The Dictations")
- *Maqasid al-Salat* ("The Aims of Prayer"). The Sultan al-Malik al-Ashraf had it read repeatedly in his gatherings, and Shams al-Din Sibt al-Jawzi exhorted people from the pulpit to teach it to their children.
- *al-Fatawa al-Mawsiliyya* ("Legal Responses of Mosul")
- *al-Fatawa al-Misriyya* ("Legal Responses of Egypt")
- *Shajara al-Ma'arif* ("The Tree of the Sciences")
- *Majaz al-Qur'an* ("The Metaphors of the Qur'an")
- *Bayan Ahwal Yawm al-Qiyama* ("Exposition of the Conditions of the Day of Judgment")
- Among his short epistles in doctrine: *al-Mulha fi I'tiqad Ahl al-Haqq* ("The Fair Speech Concerning the Belief of the People of Truth"), *al-Anwa' fi 'Ilm al-Tawhid* ("The Various Branches in the Science of Oneness"), *Risala fi al-Tawhid* ("Epistle on Oneness"), *al-Wasiyya* ("The Testament")
- *Mukhtasar al-Ri'aya*, an abridgment of al-Muhasibi's *Kitab al-Ri'aya li Huquq Allah* ("Book of Observance of the Rights of Allah")
- *Risala fi al-Qutb wa al-Abdal al-Arba'in* ("Treatise on the Pole of Saints and the Forty Substitutes")

---

[26] Ibn 'Abd al-Salam, *Fatawa* (p. 138-142).

- *Fawa'id al-Balwa wa al-Mihan* ("The Benefits of Trials and Afflictions")
- *Nihaya al-Rughba fi Adab al-Suhba* ("The Obtainment of Wishes in the Etiquette of Companionship")
- *Al-Farq Bayn al-Iman wa al-Islam* ("The Difference Between Belief and Submission")

Among Ibn 'Abd al-Salam's legacies in *usûl* and the hadith sciences is the following rule described by the hadith master al-Sakhawi:

I have heard my shaykh [Ibn Hajar] insist on the following, and he put it to me in writing himself, namely: The conditions for any practice based on weak hadith are three:

1. That the weakness not be very strong. This condition is agreed upon. This excludes those hadiths singly recorded by liars or those accused of lying, and by those who make gross mistakes.
2. That there be a general legal basis for it. This excludes what is invented and has no legal basis to start with.
3. That one not think, when practicing on the basis of it, that the hadith in question is actually established as sound. This is to preclude the attribution to the Prophet 🌙 of words he did not say.

The last two conditions are from Ibn 'Abd al-Salam and his companion Ibn Daqiq al-'Id, while Abu Sa'id al-'Ala'i reported unanimity over the first one.[27]

Imam al-Shafi'i 🌙 (d. 204)

Muhammad ibn Idris ibn al-'Abbas, al-Imam al-Shafi'i, Abu 'Abd Allah al-Shafi'i al-Hijazi al-Qurashi al-Hashimi al-Muttalibi, the offspring of the House of the Prophet 🌙, the peerless one of the great *mujtahid* imams and jurisprudent *par excellence*, the scrupulously pious ascetic and

---

[27]Al-Sakhawi, last chapter of *al-Qawl al-Badi' fi al-Salat wa al-Salam 'ala al-Shafi'*. The material in this section is from Al-Dhahabi, *Siyar* (17:33); Ibn al-Subki, *Tabaqat al-Shafi'iyya al-Kubra* (8:209-255 #1183); Ibn Kathir, *al-Bidaya wa al-Nihaya* (13:273); Ibn 'Imad, *Shadharat al-Dhahab* (5:301-302).

Friend of Allah, he laid down the foundations of *fiqh* in his *Risala*, which he said he revised and re-read four hundred times, then said: "Only Allah's Book is perfect and free from error."

He is the cousin of the Prophet ﷺ descending from al-Muttalib who is the brother of Hashim, 'Abd al-Muttalib's father. Someone praised the Banu Hashim in front of the Prophet ﷺ, whereupon the latter interlaced the fingers of his two hands and said: "We and they are but one and the same thing."[28] Al-Nawawi listed three peculiar merits of al-Shafi'i: his sharing the Prophet's ﷺ lineage at the level of their common ancestor 'Abd Manaf; his birth in the Holy Land of Palestine and upbringing in Mecca; and his education at the hands of superlative scholars together with his own superlative intelligence and knowledge of the Arabic language. To this Ibn Hajar added two more: the hadith of the Prophet ﷺ, "O Allah! Guide Quraysh, for the science of the scholar that comes from them will encompass the earth. O Allah! You have let the first of them taste bitterness, so let the latter of them taste reward."[29] Another hadith of the Prophet ﷺ says: "Truly, Allah shall send forth for this Community, at the onset of every hundred years, someone who will renew their Religion for them."[30] The scholars agreed, among them Abu Qilaba (d. 276) and Imam Ahmad, that the first narration signified al-Shafi'i,[31] and the second signified 'Umar ibn 'Abd al-'Aziz and then al-Shafi'i.[32]

---

[28]Narrated from 'Uthman by al-Bukhari in his *Sahih*.

[29]Narrated from Abu Hurayra by al-Khatib in *Tarikh Baghdad*; from Ibn Mas'ud by Abu Dawud al-Tayalisi in his *Musnad*; from Ibn 'Abbas by al-Bayhaqi in *al-Madkhal* and al-Quda'i; and from 'Ali by al-Hakim and al-Abiri, and from all four Companions by Ibn Hajar in *Tawali al-Ta'sis*, all with weak chains which, al-Bayhaqi and Ibn Hajar said, if collated, make the hadith strong. The second sentence is narrated alone from Ibn 'Abbas by Tirmidhi who said it is *hasan sahih gharib*, and by Ahmad with a good chain according to Ibn Hajar in *Tawali al-Ta'sis* (p. 44), sound according to Shaykh Ahmad Shakir in his edition of the *Musnad* (2:553 #2170), and fair according to al-Ahdab in *Zawa'id Tarikh Baghdad* (1:490).

[30]Narrated from Abu Hurayra by Abu Dawud in his *Sunan*, al-Hakim in the *Mustadrak*, and others, with a strong chain as stated by Ibn Hajar in *Tawali al-Ta'sis* (p. 49).

[31]As narrated in al-Mizzi's *Tahdhib al-Kamal* (3:22 #1162) and Ibn Hajar's *Tawali al-Ta'sis* (p. 45).

[32]As narrated in al-Bayhaqi's *Manaqib al-Shafi'i* (1:54), Ibn Hajar's *Tawali al-Ta'sis* (p. 47-49), al-'Ajluni's *Kashf al-Khafa'*, and elsewhere.

He was born in Ghazza or 'Asqalan in 150, the year of Abu Hanifa's death, and moved to Mecca at the age of two, following his father's death, where he grew up. He was early a skillful archer, then he took to learning language and poetry until he gave himself to *fiqh*, beginning with hadith. He memorized the Qur'an at age seven, then Malik's *Muwatta'* at age ten, at which time his teacher would deputize him to teach in his absence. At age thirteen he went to see Malik, who was impressed by his memory and intelligence.

Malik ibn Anas and Muhammad ibn al-Hasan al-Shaybani were among his most prominent teachers and he took position against both of them in *fiqh*. Al-Shafi'i said: "From Muhammad ibn al-Hasan I wrote a camel-load." Al-Hakim narrated from 'Abd Allah ibn 'Abd al-Hakam: "Al-Shafi'i never ceased to speak according to Malik's position and he would say: 'We do not differ from him other than in the way of his companions,' until some young men spoke unbecomingly at length behind his back, whereupon al-Shafi'i resolved to put his differences with Malik in writing. Otherwise, his whole life he would say, whenever asked something: 'This is what the Teacher said' – *hâdha qawl al-ustâdh* – meaning Malik."[33]

Like Abu Hanifa and al-Bukhari, he recited the entire Qur'an each day at prayer, and twice a day in the month of Ramadan.

Al-Muzani said: "I never saw one more handsome of face than al-Shafi'i. If he grasped his beard it would not exceed his fist." Ibn Rahuyah described him in Mecca as wearing bright white clothes with an intensely black beard. Al-Za'farani said that when he was in Baghdad in the year 195 he dyed his beard with henna.

Abu 'Ubayd al-Qasim ibn Sallam said: "If the intelligence of an entire nation was brought together he would have encompassed it." Similarly, al-Muzani said: "I have been looking into al-Shafi'i's *Risala* for fifty years, and I do not recall a single time I looked at it without learning some new benefit."

Al-Sakhawi in the introduction to his *al-Jawahir wa al-Durar* and others narrate that someone criticized Ahmad ibn Hanbal for attending the

---

[33]Ibn Hajar, *Tawali al-Ta'sis* p. 153-154.

fiqh sessions of al-Shafi'i and leaving the hadith sessions of Sufyan ibn 'Uyayna. Ahmad replied: "Keep quiet! If you miss a hadith with a shorter chain you can find it elsewhere with a longer chain and it will not harm you. But if you do not have the reasoning of this man [al-Shafi'i], I fear you will never be able to find it elsewhere." Ahmad is also related by his students Abu Talib and Humayd ibn Zanjuyah to say: "I never saw anyone adhere more to hadith than al-Shafi'i. No-one preceded him in writing down the hadith in a book." The meaning of this is that al-Shafi'i possessed the understanding of hadith after which Ahmad sought, as evidenced by the latter's statement: "How rare is *fiqh* among the scholars of hadith!"[34] This is a reference to the hadith: "It may be one carries understanding *(fiqh)* without being a person of understanding *(faqih)*."[35] Sufyan himself would defer to al-Shafi'i in matters of *tafsir* and *fatwa*. Yunus ibn Abi Ya'la said: "Whenever al-Shafi'i went into *tafsir*, it was as if he had witnessed the revelation." Ahmad ibn Hanbal also said: "Not one of the scholars of hadith touched an inkwell nor a pen except he owed a huge debt to al-Shafi'i."

A notable position of al-Shafi'i and his school is the reading of the *basmala* -- ❴IN THE NAME OF ALLAH, THE ALL-BENEFICENT, THE MOST MERCIFUL❵ (1:1) as the first verse of sura al-Fatiha and of every sura of the Qur'an except the ninth (al-Tawba). This position was discussed, among others, by Shaykh al-Islam Zayn al-Din al-'Iraqi.[36]

Al-Shafi'i was known for his peculiar strength in Arabic language, poetry, and philology. Bayhaqi narrated:

> [From Ibn Hisham:] I was al-Shafi'i's sitting-companion for a long time, and I never heard him use except a word which, carefully considered, one would not find (in its context) a better word in the entire Arabic language. . . . Al-Shafi'i's discourse, in relation to language, is a proof in itself.

---

[34] Cited by Shaykh 'Abd al-Fattah Abu Ghudda in his introduction to Muhammad al-Shaybani's *Muwatta'*.
[35] A nearly-mass-narrated *(mashhur)* sound hadith of the Prophet ﷺ reported from several Companions by al-Tirmidhi, Abu Dawud, Ibn Majah, and Ahmad.
[36] In his book *Tarh al-Tathrib* (4:189-190).

[From al-Hasan ibn Muhammad al-Za'farani:] A group of bedouins used to frequent al-Shafi'i's gathering with us and sit in a corner. One day I asked their leader: "You are not interested in scholarship; why do you keep coming to sit with us?" They said: "We come to hear al-Shafi'i's language."[37]

Al-Shafi'i trod the path of the *Salaf* in avoiding any interpretation of the verses and narrations pertaining to the divine attributes. He practiced "relegation of the meaning" *(tafwîd al-ma'na)* to a higher source, as established in his saying: "I leave the meaning of the verses of the Attributes to Allah, and I leave the meaning of the hadiths of the attributes to Allah's Messenger ﷺ." At the same time, rare instances of interpretation are recorded from him. Thus al-Bayhaqi relates that al-Muzani reported from al-Shafi'i the following commentary on the verse: ❴**To Allah belong the East and the West, and wheresoever you turn, there is Allah's face** *(wajh)*❵ (2:115): "It means – and Allah knows best – thither is the bearing *(wajh)* towards which Allah has directed you."[38] Al-Hakkari (d. 486) related in his book *'Aqida al-Shafi'i* that the latter said: "We affirm those attributes, and we negate from them likeness between them and creation *(al-tashbîh)*, just as He negated it from Himself when He said: ❴**There is nothing whatsoever like unto Him**❵ (42:11)."

Al-Shafi'i's hatred of dialectic theology *(kalâm)* was based on his extreme caution against errors which bear heavy consequences as they induce one into false beliefs. Among his sayings concerning this: "It is better for a scholar of knowledge to give a *fatwâ* after which he is said to be wrong than to theologize and then be said to be a heretic *(zindîq)*. I hate nothing more than theology and theologians." Dhahabi comments: "This indicates that Abu 'Abd Allah's position concerning error in the tenets of faith *(al-usûl)* is that it is not the same as error in the course of scholarly exertion in the branches." The reason is that in belief and doctrine neither *ijtihâd* nor *ikhtilâf* are permitted. In this respect al-Shafi'i said: "It cannot be asked 'Why?' concerning the principles, nor 'How?'" Yet al-Shafi'i

---

[37]Al-Bayhaqi *Manaqib al-Shafi'i* (2:42-46).

[38]Bayhaqi continues: "The hadith master Abu 'Abd Allah [al-Hakim] and the hadith master al-Qadi Abu Bakr ibn al-'Arabi have related to us from Mujahid that he said regarding this verse: "It means the direction of prayer to Allah *(qibla)*, therefore wheresoever you are, East and West, do not turn your faces except towards it."

did not completely close the door to the use of *kalâm* in defense of the Sunna, as shown below and in the notice on Ahmad ibn Hanbal.

Yunus ibn Abi Ya‘la narrated that al-Shafi‘i defined the "principles" as: "The Qur'an, the Sunna, analogy *(al-qiyâs)*, and consensus *(al-ijmâ‘)*"; he defined the latter to mean: "The adherence of the Congregation *(jamâ‘a)* of the Muslims to the conclusions of a given ruling pertaining to what is permitted and what is forbidden after the Prophet's 鱉 passing."

Al-Shafi‘i did not close the door on the right use of *kalâm* as is clear from Ibn Abi Hatim's narration from al-Rabi‘ of his words: "If I wished, I could produce a book against each one of those who deviated, but dialectic theology is none of my business, and I would not like to be attributed any part in it."[39] Similar to it is his advice to his student al-Muzani: "Take proofs from creation about the Creator, and do not burden yourself with the knowledge of what your mind did not reach." Ibn Abi Hatim himself spoke similarly when he was told of Ibn Khuzayma's unsuccessful attempt at *kalâm*: "It is preferable not to meddle with what we did not learn." This is similar to Imam Malik's preference not to speak about other than what relates to practice.[40] Note that al-Shafi‘i also spoke of his wish not to have a single letter out of all his works attributed to him, regardless of topic.

Al-Shafi‘i's attitude towards *tasawwuf* was as strict as with *kalâm*, and he both praised it and denigrated its abuse at the hands of its corrupters. In criticism of the latter he said: "No-one becomes a Sufi in the morning except he ends up a dolt by noon" while on the other hand he declared in his *Diwan*: "Be at the same time a *faqîh* and a Sufi." In Mecca al-Shafi‘i was the student of Fudayl ibn ‘Iyad. Imam al-Nawawi in his *Bustan al-‘Arifin fi al-Zuhd wa al-Tasawwuf* ("The Garden of the Gnostics in Asceticism and *Tasawwuf*") narrated from al-Shafi‘i the saying: "Only the sincere one *(al-mukhlis)* can recognize self-display *(al-riyâ')*." Al-Nawawi comments: "This means that it is impossible to know the reality of self-display and see its hidden shades except for one who resolutely seeks *(arâda)* sincerity. Such a one strives for a long time, searching, meditating, examining at length within himself until he knows, or knows something of what self-display is. This does not happen for

---

[39]Al-Dhahabi said: "This breath of fresh air is mass-narrated from the Imam."
[40]See below, n. 138.

everyone. Indeed, this happens only with special ones *(al-khawâss)*. But for a given individual to claim that he knows what self-diplay is, this is real ignorance on his part."

Al-Shafi'i deferred primacy in the foundations of *fiqh* to Imam Abu Hanifa with his famous statement: "People are all the children of Abu Hanifa in *fiqh*." Ibn Hajar al-Haytami mentioned in the thirty-fifth chapter of his book on Imam Abu Hanifa entitled *al-Khayrat al-Hisan*: "When Imam al-Shafi'i was in Baghdad, he would visit the grave of Imam Abu Hanifa, greet him, and then ask Allah for the fulfillment of his need through his means."

Two schools of legal thought or *madhahib* are actually attributed to al-Shafi'i, englobing his writings and legal opinions *(fatâwa)*. These two schools are known in the terminology of jurists as "The Old" *(al-qadîm)* and "The New" *(al-jadîd)*, corresponding respectively to his stays in Iraq and Egypt. The most prominent transmitters of the New among al-Shafi'i's students are al-Buwayti,[41] al-Muzani, al-Rabi' al-Muradi, and al-Bulqini, in *Kitab al-Umm* ("The Motherbook"). The most prominent transmitters of the Old are Ahmad ibn Hanbal, al-Karabisi, al-Za'farani, and Abu Thawr, in *Kitab al-Hujja* ("Book of the Proof"). What is presently known as the Shafi'i position refers to the New except in approximately twenty-two questions, in which Shafi'i scholars and muftis have retained the positions of the Old.

Ibn al-Subki related that the Shafi'i scholars considered al-Rabi's narration from al-Shafi'i sounder from the viewpoint of transmission, while they considered al-Muzani's sounder from the viewpoint of *fiqh*, although both were established hadith masters. Al-Shafi'i said to al-Rabi': "How I love you!" and another time: "O Rabi'! If I could feed you the Science I would feed it to you." Al-Qaffal al-Shashi in his *Fatawa* relates that al-Rabi' was slow in his understanding, and that al-Shafi'i once repeated an explanation forty times for him in a gathering, yet he did not understand it then got up and left in embarrassment. Later, al-Shafi'i called him in private and resumed explaining it to him until he understood.

---

[41]Al-Shafi'i named him the most knowledgeable person in his school. He died in 231 in jail, bound in chains in Iraq for refusing to say that the Qur'an was created. May Allah have mercy on him and on all the scholars of *Ahl al-Sunna*. SAN (10:67-69 #1978).

This shows the accuracy of Ibn Rahuyah's statement: "I consider the best part of me the time when I fully understand al-Shafi'i's discourse."

Al-Shafi'i took the verse **《Or if you have touched women》** (4:43) literally, and considered that contact between the sexes, even accidental, nullified ablution. This is also the position of Ibn Mas'ud, Ibn 'Umar, al-Sha'bi, al-Nakha'i, al-Zuhri, and al-Awza'i, which is confirmed by Ibn 'Umar's report: "Whoever kisses or touches his wife with his hand must renew his *wudû'*." It is authentic and related in numerous places including Malik's *Muwatta'*. Al-Shafi'i said: "Something similar has reached us from Ibn Mas'ud." They all read the above verse literally, without interpreting "touch" to mean "sexual intercourse" as do the Hanafis, or "touch with pleasure" as do the Malikis.

A major contribution of al-Shafi'i in the foundations of the Law was his division of innovation *(al-bid'a)* into good and bad on the basis of 'Umar's words about the *tarâwih* or congregational supererogatory night prayers in the month of Ramadan: "What a fine innovation this is!"[42] Harmala narrated that al-Shafi'i concluded: "Therefore, whatever innovation conforms to the Sunna is approved *(mahmûd)*, and whatever opposes it is abominable *(madhmûm)*."[43] Agreement formed in the Four Schools around his division, as illustrated by the endorsement of some major later authorities in each school. Among the Hanafis: Ibn 'Abidin, al-Turkumani, and al-Tahanawi;[44] among the Malikis: al-Turtushi, Ibn al-Hajj, and al-Shatibi;[45] consensus among the Shafi'is;[46] and reluctant

---

[42]Narrated by Malik in *al-Muwatta'* and al-Bukhari in his *Sahih*.

[43]Narrated by Abu Nu'aym with his chain through Abu Bakr al-Ajurri in *Hilya al-Awliya'* (9:121 #13315) and by al-Bayhaqi in his *Madkhal* and *Manaqib al-Shafi'i* (1:469) with a sound chain, as stated by Ibn Taymiyya in his *Dar' Ta'arud al-'Aql wa al-Naql* (p. 171).

[44]Ibn 'Abidin, *Hashiya* (1:376); al-Turkumani, *Kitab al-Luma' fi al-Hawadith wa al-Bida'* (Stuttgart, 1986, 1:37); al-Tahanawi, *Kashshaf Istilahat al-Funun* (Beirut, 1966, 1:133-135).

[45]Al-Turtushi, *Kitab al-Hawadith wa al-Bida'* (p. 158-159); Ibn al-Hajj, *Madkhal al-Shar' al-Sharif* (Cairo, 1336H 2:115); al-Shatibi, *Kitab al-I'tisam* (Beirut ed. 1:188).

[46]Abu Shama, *al-Ba'ith 'ala Inkar al-Bida' wa al-Hawadith* (Riyad: Dar al-Raya, 1990 p. 93, Cairo ed. p. 12); al-'Izz ibn 'Abd al-Salam, as mentioned by the following; al-Nawawi, *al-Adhkar* (Beirut: al-Thaqafiyya, p. 237), and *Tahdhib al-Asma' wa al-Lughat* (3:22); Ibn Hajar, *Fath al-Bari* (13:253-254); al-Suyuti, introduction to *Husn al-Maqsid fi 'Amal al-Mawlid* in *al-Hawi li al-Fatawi*. Etc.

acceptance among later Hanbalis, who altered al-Shafi'i's terminology to read "lexical innovation" *(bid'a lughawiyya)* and "legal innovation" *(bid'a shar'iyya)*, respectively – although inaccurately – matching Shafi'i's "approved" and "abominable".[47]

Among al-Shafi'i's other notable positions: Al-Muzani said: "I never saw any of the scholars make something obligatory on behalf of the Prophet 🌱 as much as al-Shafi'i in his books, and this was due to his high remembrance of the Prophet 🌱. He said in the Old School: 'Supplication ends with the invocation of blessings on the Prophet 🌱, and its end is but by means of it.'" Al-Karabisi said: "I heard al-Shafi'i say that he disliked for someone to say 'the Messenger' *(al-Rasûl)*, but that he should say 'Allah's Messenger' *(Rasûlullâh)* out of veneration *(ta'zîm)* for him."

Among al-Shafi'i's other sayings:

- "The study of hadith is better than supererogatory prayer, and the pursuit of knowledge is better than supererogatory prayer." Ibn 'Abd al-Barr in *Kitab al-'Ilm* listed the many hadiths of the Prophet 🌱 on the superior merit of knowledge. However, al-Shafi'i by this saying meant the essence and purpose of knowledge, not knowledge for its own sake which leads to Satanic pride. The latter is widely available while true knowledge is the knowledge that leads to godwariness *(taqwâ)*. This is confirmed by al-Shafi'i's saying: "Knowledge is what benefits. Knowledge is not what one has memorized." This is a corrective for those content to define knowledge as "the knowledge of the proof" *(ma'rifa al-dalîl)*. ⟨He gives wisdom to whomever He will, and whoever receives wisdom receives immense good⟩ (2:269).[48]

Note that "consensus" *(ijmâ')* is more inclusive than "agreement" *(ittifâq)*, and binding.

[47]Ibn Rajab, *al-Jami' fi al-'Ulum wa al-Hikam* (2:50-53), and Ibn Taymiyya's section on *bid'a* in his *Iqtida' al-Sirat al-Mustaqim Mukhalafa Ashab al-Jahim*. This is also the position of Ibn Kathir: see his commentary of the verse: ⟨The Originator of the heavens and the earth!⟩ (2:117) in his *Tafsir*. He followed in this his teacher Ibn Taymiyya.

[48]See also the following definitions of *fiqh*, wisdom, knowledge, and reason: Al-Hasan al-Basri said: "Have you ever seen a *faqîh*? The *faqîh* is he who has renounced the world, longs for the hereafter, possesses insight in his Religion, and worships his Lord without cease." As cited by al-'Ayni in *'Umda al-Qari*, Book of *'Ilm*, in his

commentary on the hadith: "He for whom Allah desires great good, He grants him understanding in the Religion," and Ibn al-Jawzi, *Manaqib al-Hasan al-Basri* (p. 16). Imam Malik: "Wisdom is superlative understanding *(al-fiqh)* in Allah's Religion." As cited by al-Tabari in his *Tafsir* (verse 21:79) and al-Mahdawi in *al-Tahsil* as quoted by Hamid Lahmar in *al-Imam Malik Mufassiran* (p. 279). Al-Tustari: "The best knowledge is that which one acts upon." Ibn Abi Ya'la, *Tabaqat al-Hanabila* (2:18); "No-one is given a better knowledge than that by which he increases his utter dependence on Allah." Abu Nu'aym, *Hilya al-Awliya'* (10:204 #14934). Ibn Hibban (al-Arna'ut, Introduction to Ibn Hibban's *Sahih*): "Knowledge" means "knowledge of the Sunna" in the Prophet's ﷺ hadith "Time shall grow short and knowledge decrease," in view of the increase of every other type of knowledge in modern times. [The hadith is part of a longer narration from Abu Hurayra by al-Bukhari, Muslim, Abu Dawud, and Ibn Majah.] "Reason *(al-'aql)* is one of different types of necessary types of knowledge that characterize animate beings endowed with speech, and its seat is the heart." Ahmad ibn Hanbal in *Tabaqat al-Hanabila* (2:281). "Lexically, 'reason' *(al-'aql)* means 'the prevention' *(al-man')*, as it prevents its owner from straying from the correct path. Conventionally, it is an instinct *(ghariza)* through which one is prepared to comprehend the theoretical sciences. It is also said to be a light cast into the heart." Zakariyya al-Ansari, *al-Hudud al-Aniqa* (p. 67).

Related to Malik's words, note the Prophet's ﷺ hadith: "Most of the people of Paradise are the naïve *(al-bulh)*." Narrated from Anas by al-Bazzar in his *Musnad* (#1983) who graded it weak, while al-Qurtubi declared it *sahih* in his *Tafsir* (verses 26:83-89), but this was questioned by al-'Iraqi in *al-Mughni 'an Haml al-Asfar*, who quoted Ibn 'Adi's rejection of the hadith in *al-Kamil fi al-Du'afa'* (3:313 #773). Ibn 'Adi said "condemned as narrated through this chain" *(hâdha al-hadîth bi hâdha al-isnâd munkarun)*, and did not mean the content of the hadith, as its veracity is confirmed by the Prophet's ﷺ hadith narrated from Abu Hurayra by Muslim: "Paradise says: None enters me except the weak and wretched among the people and their simple-minded *(ghirratuhum)*." The best grading for the chain of Anas's narration is that of "soft" *(layyin)* in al-Fattani's *Tadhkira al-Mawdu'at* (p. 29) and al-'Ajluni's *Kashf al-Khafa'* (1:164, 1:286) because of Salama ibn Rawh. See also al-Mizzi's *Tahdhib al-Kamal* (26:113 #5465), al-Quda'i's *Musnad al-Shihab* (2:110 #989-990), al-Suyuti's *al-Durar al-Muntathira* (p. 93 #68), al-Sakhawi's *al-Maqasid al-Hasana* (p. 74), and al-Zarkashi's *al-Tadhkira* (p. 170). The hadith is also narrated with a weak chain from Jabir as stated by Ibn 'Adi (1:191 #31), Ibn al-Jawzi in *al-'Ilal al-Mutanahiya* (2:934-935 #1558-1559), and Ibn Hajar in *Lisan al-Mizan* (1:240 #755). The *ghirr* and *bulh* are those who were ignorant of evil ways in the world but knowledgeable in their Religion, as explained by Abu 'Uthman and al-Awza'i in *Kashf al-Khafa'* and al-Munawi in *Fayd al-Qadir* (2:79); or those whose hearts were guileless towards people as stated by Ibn Qutayba in *Ta'wil Mukhtalaf al-Hadith* (1995 ed. p. 270, 1972 ed. p. 297); or those who lacked skill in worldly ways as explained by al-Nawawi in *Sharh Sahih Muslim* and al-Suyuti in *al-Dibaj* (6:191 #2847); or those like old women, beduins, and their like, who remained staunch in their Religion as stated by al-Qari in *Al-Asrar al-Marfu'a* (p. 125-127 #53). The "Salafi" editor of the latter, M.L. al-Sabbagh, rejected the hadith as *munkar* and

- "You [the scholars of hadith] are the pharmacists but we [the jurists] are the physicians." This was explained by 'Ali al-Qari in his book *Mu'taqad Abi Hanifa al-Imam* (p. 42): "The early scholars said: The hadith scholar without knowledge of *fiqh* is like a seller of drugs who is no physician: he has them but he does not know what to do with them; and the *fiqh* scholar without knowledge of hadith is like a physician without drugs: he knows what constitutes a remedy, but does not dispose of it."

- "Malik was asked about *kalâm* and [the Science of] Oneness *(tawhîd)* and he said: 'It is inconceivable that the Prophet ﷺ should teach his Community hygiene and not teach them about Oneness! And Oneness is exactly what the Prophet ﷺ said: 'I was ordered to fight people until they say 'There is no God but Allah.'[49] So, whatever makes blood and property untouchable – that is the reality of Oneness *(haqiqa al-tawhîd)*.'" This is a proof from the *Salaf* against those who, in later times, innovated sub-divisions for *tawhîd* or legislated that their own understanding of Allah's Attributes was a precondition for the declaration of Oneness. Al-Bayhaqi mentioned al-Halimi's inference from the same hadith: "In this hadith there is explicit proof that that declaration *(lâ ilâha illallâh)* suffices to extirpate oneself from all the different kinds of disbelief in Allah Almighty."[50]

- "Satiation weighs down the body, hardens the heart, does away with sagacity, brings on sleep, and weakens one from worship."

---

exclaimed: "Islam was never for one day a Religion that supports naiveness or the simple-minded!" This is refuted by Muslim's narration from Abu Hurayra quoted above, as well as al-Tirmidhi *(gharîb)*, Abu Dawud, Ahmad, al-Hakim (1:43), and 'Abd al-Razzaq's narration from him that the Prophet ﷺ said: "The believer is guileless and noble *(al-mu'minu ghirrun karim)* while the wicked man is perfidious and miserly *(wa al-fâjiru khibbun la'im)*": a fair narration as indicated by al-Dhahabi in his *Talkhis* and stated by Ibn Hajar in *al-Ajwiba 'ala al-Qazwini* [in al-Qari's *Mirqat* 1994 ed. 1:546-549] and al-Suyuti as quoted in *'Awn al-Ma'bud*. Al-Bayhaqi also narrated from Abu Hurayra, as stated in al-Qari's *al-Mirqat* (1994 ed. 8:813): "The believer is easy and lenient *(hayyinun layyinun)* to the point that you will think him a fool *(ahmaq)* in his leniency." Ibn al-Athir cites some of these narrations under the entries *b-l-h* and *gh-r-r* in *al-Nihaya* (1:154, 3:353), as well as Muhammad ibn Abi Bakr al-Razi in *Mukhtar al-Sihah* (p. 26).

[49] A mass-narrated *(mutawâtir)* hadith of the Prophet ﷺ narrated by Bukhari, Muslim, and others from nineteen Companions as stated by al-Kattani in *Nazm al-Mutanathir*.
[50] Al-Bayhaqi, *al-Asma' wa al-Sifat* (al-Kawthari ed. p. 96; al-Hashidi ed. 1:235).

This is similar to the definition of *tasawwuf* as "hunger" *(al-jū')* given by some of the early masters, who acquired hunger as a permanent attribute and were called "hungerers" *(jū'iyyūn)*. Notable examples are Sahl ibn 'Abd Allah al-Tustari and al-Qasim ibn 'Uthman al-'Abdi al-Dimashqi al-Ju'i (d. 248).[51]

- "I never swore by Allah – neither truthfully nor deceptively." The Sufi master Sahl ibn 'Abd Allah al-Tustari said something similar.

- Al-Buwayti asked: "Should I pray behind the *Rafidi*?" Al-Shafi'i said: "Do not pray behind the *Rafidi*, nor behind the *Qadari*, nor behind the *Murji'*." Al-Buwayti said: "Define them for us." He replied: "Whoever says 'Belief consists only in speech' is a *Murji'*, and whoever says 'Abu Bakr and 'Umar are not Imams' is a *Rafidi*, and whoever attributes destiny to himself is a *Qadari*."

Abu Hatim al-Razi narrated from Harmala that al-Shafi'i said: "The [Rightly-Guided] Caliphs are five: Abu Bakr, 'Umar, 'Uthman, 'Ali, and 'Umar ibn 'Abd al-'Aziz." In his *Diwan* he named them "leaders of their people, by whose guidance one obtains guidance," and declaimed of the Family of the Prophet ﷺ:

The Family of the Prophet are my intermediary to him! (wasilati)
Through them I hope to be given my record with the right hand.

and:

O Family of Allah's Messenger! To love you is an obligation
Which Allah ordained and revealed in the Qur'an.
It is enough proof of your immense glory that
Whoever invokes not blessings upon you, his prayer is invalid.

Ibn Hajar said that the first to write a biography of al-Shafi'i was Dawud al-Zahiri (d. 275). Al-Nawawi mentioned that the best biography of al-Shafi'i was al-Bayhaqi's for its sound chains of transmission.[52] Ibn

---

[51]Al-Dhahabi described the latter as "the Imam, the exemplar, the *walī*, the *muhaddith*, the shaykh of the Sufis and the friend of Ahmad ibn al-Hawari." 'Abd Allah ibn 'Umar said: "I never ate to satiation since I entered Islam." Abu Nu'aym, *Hilya* (1:371 #1031).
[52]In *Tahdhib al-Asma' wa al-Lughat* (1:44).

Hajar summarized it and added to it al-Shafi'i's *Musnad* in his *Tawali al-Ta'sis fi Ma'ali Ibn Idris.*

In the introduction of his great compendium of Shafi'i *fiqh* entitled *al-Majmu'* al-Nawawi mentioned that al-Shafi'i used a walking stick. One day he was asked: "Why do you carry a stick when you are neither old nor ailing?" He replied: "To remind myself that I am only a traveller in this world."[53]

Imam Ahmad ibn Hanbal  (d. 241)

Ahmad ibn Muhammad ibn Hanbal, Abu 'Abd Allah al-Dhuhli al-Shaybani al-Marwazi al-Baghdadi. Al-Dhahabi says of him: "The true Shaykh of Islam and leader of the Muslims in his time, the hadith master and proof of the Religion. He took hadith from Hushaym, Ibrahim ibn Sa'd, Sufyan ibn 'Uyayna, 'Abbad ibn 'Abbad, Yahya ibn Abi Za'ida, and their layer. From him narrated al-Bukhari [two hadiths in the *Sahih*], Muslim [22], Abu Dawud [254], Abu Zur'a, Mutayyan, 'Abd Allah ibn Ahmad, Abu al-Qasim al-Baghawi, and a huge array of scholars. His father was a soldier – one of those who called to Islam – and he died young." Al-Dhahabi continues:

- 'Abd Allah ibn Ahmad said: "I heard Abu Zur'a [al-Razi] say: 'Your father had memorized a million hadiths, which I rehearsed with him according to topic.'"[54]

- Hanbal said: "I heard Abu 'Abd Allah say: 'I memorized everything which I heard from Hushaym when he was alive.'"

- Ibrahim al-Harbi said: "I held Ahmad as one for whom Allah had gathered up the combined knowledge of the first and the last."

---

[53] Al-Shafi'i, *Diwan*; Abu Nu'aym, *Hilya al-Awliya'* (9:71-172 #442); al-Nawawi, *Tahdhib al-Asma' wa al-Lughat* (1:44-67 #2); al-Dhahabi, *Siyar A'lam al-Nubala'* (8:377-423 #1539, 10:79, 10:649); Ibn al-Subki, *Tabaqat al-Shafi'iyya al-Kubra* (2:133-134); Ibn Hajar, *Tawali al-Ta'sis* (p. 3-157).
[54] By the phrase "a million hadiths" are meant the chains of transmission, as the hadith texts themselves, without repetition, do not exceed ten thousand sound hadiths according to the hadith masters.

- Harmala said: "I heard al-Shafi'i say: 'I left Baghdad and did not leave behind me anyone more virtuous *(afdal)*, more learned *(a'lam)*, more knowledgeable *(afqah)* than Ahmad ibn Hanbal.'"

- 'Ali ibn al-Madini said: "Truly, Allah reinforced this Religion with Abu Bakr al-Siddiq ﷺ the day of the Great Apostasy *(al-Ridda)*, and He reinforced it with Ahmad ibn Hanbal ﷺ at the time of the ordeal *(al-mihna)*."

- Abu 'Ubayd said: "The Science at its peak is in the custody of four men, of whom Ahmad ibn Hanbal is the most knowledgeable."

- Ibn Ma'in said, as related by 'Abbas [al-Duri]: "They meant for me to be like Ahmad, but – by Allah! – I shall never in my life compare to him."

- Muhammad ibn Hammad al-Taharani said: "I heard Abu Thawr say: 'Ahmad is more learned – or knowledgeable – than al-Thawri.'"

- Zakariyya ibn Yahya al-Darir said to Imam Ahmad: "How many memorized hadiths are sufficient for someone to be a mufti? Are one hundred thousand sufficient?" He said no. "Two hundred thousand?" He said no. "Three?" He said no, until Zakariyya said: "Five hundred thousand?" Ahmad said: "I hope that that should be sufficient."

Al-Dhahabi concludes: "Al-Bayhaqi wrote Ahmad's biography *(sîra)* in one volume, so did Ibn al-Jawzi, and also *Shaykh al-Islam*[55] ['Abd Allah al-Harawi] al-Ansari in a brief volume. He passed on to Allah's good pleasure on the day of *Jum'a*, the twelfth of *Rabi' al-Awwal* in the year 241, at the age of seventy-seven. I have two of his short-chained narrations *('awâlîh)*, and a licence *(ijâza)* for the entire *Musnad*." Dhahabi's chapter on Imam Ahmad in *Siyar A'lam al-Nubala'* counts no less than 113 pages.

One of the misunderstandings prevalent among the "Salafis" who misrepresent Imam Ahmad's school today is his position regarding *kalâm* or dialectic theology. It is known that he was uncompromisingly opposed to *kalâm* as a method, even if used as a means to defend the truth,

---

[55]See Appendix, "The Title: *Shaykh al-Islam*."

preferring to stick to the plain narration of textual proofs and abandoning all recourse to dialectical or rational ones. Ibn al-Jawzi relates his saying: "Do not sit with the people of *kalâm*, even if they defend the Sunna." This attitude is at the root of his disavowal of al-Muhasibi. It also explains the disaffection of later Hanbalis towards Imam al-Ash'ari and his school, despite the latter's subsequent standing as the Imam of Sunni Muslims *par excellence*. The reasons for this rift are now obsolete although the rift has amplified beyond all recognizable shape, as it is evident, in retrospect, that opposition to Ash'aris, for various reasons, came out of a major misunderstanding of their actual contributions within the Community, whether as individuals or as a whole.

There are several general reasons why the Hanbali-*mutakallim* rift should be considered artificial and obsolete. First, *kalâm* in its original form was an innovation in Islam *(bid'a)* against which there was unanimous opposition among *Ahl al-Sunna*. The first to use *kalâm* were true innovators opposed to the Sunna, and in the language of the early scholars *kalâm* was synonymous with the doctrines of the *Qadariyya, Murji'a, Jahmiyya, Jabriyya, Rawâfid,* and *Mu'tazila* and their multifarious subsects. This is shown by the examples Ibn Qutayba gives of *kalâm* and *mutakallimûn* in his book *Mukhtalif al-Hadith*, none of which belongs to *Ahl al-Sunna*. Similarly the adherents of *kalâm* brought up in the speech of al-Hasan al-Basri, Ibn al-Mubarak, Ibn Rahuyah, Imam al-Shafi'i and the rest of the pre-Hanbali scholars of hadith are the innovators of the above-mentioned sects, not those who later opposed them using the same methods of reasoning. The latter cannot be put in the same category. Therefore the early blames of *kalâm* cannot be applied to them in the same breath with the innovators. Imam Abu Zahra said: "Whenever you hear Abu Yusuf or Muhammad or al-Shafi'i or Ibn Hanbal and others [among the early imams] revile the science of *kalâm* and those who take knowledge by following the methods of the *mutakallimûn,* know that they only meant the *Mu'tazila* by their criticism, and the methods of the *Mu'tazila.*"[56] Similarly Shaykh 'Abd al-Wakil Durubi said: "What al-Shafi'i meant [by the prohibition of engaging in *kalâm*] was the heretical scholastic theology that proliferated in his time and put rationalistic theories ahead of the Qur'an and Sunna, not the science of theology *('ilm al-tawhîd)* by which Ash'ari and Maturidi scholars have clarified and

---

[56]Abu Zahra, *Abu Hanifa* (p. 133).

detailed the tenets of Sunni Islam, which is an important part of the Islamic sciences."[57]

Second, there is difference of opinion among the *Salaf* on the possible use of *kalām* to defend the Sunna, notwithstanding Imam Ahmad's position quoted above. One reason why they disallowed it is *wara'*: because of extreme scrupulousness against learning and practicing a discipline initiated by the enemies of the Sunna. Thus they considered *kalām* reprehensible but not forbidden, as is clear from their statements. For example, Ibn Abi Hatim narrated that al-Shafi'i said: "If I wanted to publish books refuting every single opponent [of the Sunna] I could easily do so, but *kalām* is not for me, and I dislike that anything of it be attributed to me."[58] This shows that al-Shafi'i left the door open for others to enter a field which he abstained from entering out of strict Godwariness.

Third, *kalām* is a difficult, delicate science which demands a mind above the norm. The imams forbade it as a *sadd al-dhari'a* or pre-empting measure. They rightly foresaw that unless one possessed an adequate capacity to practice it, one was courting disaster. This was the case with Ahmad's student Abu Talib, and other early Hanbalis who misinterpreted Ahmad's doctrinal positions as Bukhari himself stated. Bukhari, Ahmad, and others of the *Salaf* thus experienced first hand that one who played with *kalām* could easily lapse into heresy, innovation, or disbelief. This was made abundantly clear in Imam Malik's answer to the man who asked how Allah established Himself over the Throne: "The establishment is known, the 'how' is inconceivable, and to ask about it is an innovation!" Malik's answer is the essence of *kalām* at the same time as it warns against the misuse of *kalām*, as observed by the late Dr. Abu al-Wafa' al-Taftazani.[59] Malik's reasoning is echoed by al-Shafi'i's advice to his student al-Muzani: "Take proofs from creation in order to know about the Creator, and do not burden yourself with the knowledge of what your mind did not reach." Similarly, Ibn Khuzayma and Ibn Abi Hatim

---

[57] In *Reliance of the Traveller* (p. 9).
[58] Narrated from al-Rabi' by al-Dhahabi in the *Siyar* (8:388).
[59] See the relevant citation in the collection of essays entitled *al-Duktur Abu al-Wafa al-Taftazani, ustadhan lil-tasawwuf wa-mufakkiran Islamiyyan, 1930-1994: buhuth 'anhu wa-dirasat mahdah ilayhi: kitab tadhkari*, ed. Atif al-Iraqi (Cairo: Dar al-Hidaya, 1995).

admitted their technical ignorance of the science of *kalâm*, at the same time acknowledging its possible good use by qualified experts. As for Ibn Qutayba, he regretted his *kalâm* days and preferred to steer completely clear of it.

In conclusion, any careful reader of Islamic intellectual history can see that if the Ash'ari scholars of *kalâm* had not engaged and defeated the various theological and philosophical sects on their own terrain, the silence of *Ahl al-Sunna* might well have sealed their defeat at the hands of their opponents. This was indicated by Taj al-Din Ibn al-Subki who spoke of the obligatoriness of *kalâm* in certain specific circumstances, as opposed to its superfluousness in other times. "The use of *kalâm* in case of necessity is a legal obligation *(wâjib)*, and to keep silence about *kalâm* in case other than necessity is a *sunna*."[60]

Al-Dhahabi relates that Imam Ahmad used to seek blessings from the relics of the Prophet 鶲 and lambasts whoever would fault the practice of *tabarruk* or seeking blessings from blessed objects:

> 'Abd Allah ibn Ahmad said: "I saw my father take a hair that belonged to the Prophet 鶲, put it on his mouth, and kiss it. I believe I saw him put it on his eyes. He also dipped it in water and drank the water to obtain cure. I saw him take the Prophet's 鶲 bowl *(qas'a)*, wash it in water, and drink from it. I saw him drink Zamzam water in order to seek cure with it, and he wiped his hands and face with it." I say: Where is the quibbling critic of Imam Ahmad now? It is also authentically established that 'Abd Allah asked his father about those who touch the pommel of the Prophet's 鶲 pulpit and touch the wall of the Prophet's 鶲 room, and he said: "I do not see any harm in it." May Allah protect us and you from the opinion of the *Khawârij* and from innovations![61]

'Abd al-Malik al-Maymuni said: "I never saw Abu 'Abd Allah wearing his turban *('imâma)* except he passed it under his chin. He disliked any other manner of wearing it."[62] He also said: "I never saw anyone more immaculate nor whiter in his clothing than Ahmad."

---

[60]Ibn al-Subki, *Tabaqat al-Shafi'iyya al-Kubra* (2:230).
[61]Al-Dhahabi, *Siyar* (9:457). Ch. on Imam Ahmad, section entitled *Min âdâbih*.
[62]The same is reported from the Imam of the Prophet's 鶲 city, Malik ibn Anas.

'Asim ibn 'Isam al-Bayhaqi said: "I spent one night at Ahmad ibn Hanbal's house. He brought me a container of water. The next morning he saw the water left untouched and said: "Allah be exalted! A man who pursues the Science, yet he does not have a nightly devotion *(wird)*?"

The biographical notice on Imam Ahmad in the *Reliance of the Traveller* reads: "Out of piety, Imam Ahmad never gave a formal legal opinion *(fatwâ)* while Shafi'i was in Iraq, and when he later formulated his school of jurisprudence, he mainly drew on explicit texts from the [Qur'an], hadith, and scholarly consensus, with relatively little expansion from analogical reasoning *(qiyâs)*. He was probably the most learned in the sciences of hadith of the four great Imams of Sacred Law, and his students included many of the foremost scholars of hadith. Abu Dawud said of him: 'Ahmad's gatherings were gatherings of the afterlife: nothing of this world was mentioned. Never once did I hear him mention this-worldly things.' And Abu Zur'a said: 'Ahmad was even greater than Ishaq [Rahawayh] *(sic)* and more knowledgeable in jurisprudence. I never saw anyone more perfect than Ahmad.' He never once missed praying in the night, and used to recite the entire [Qur'an] daily. He said, 'I saw the Lord of Power in my sleep, and said, "O Lord, what is the best act through which those near to You draw nearer?" and He answered, "Through [reciting] My word, O Ahmad." I asked, "With understanding, or without?" and He answered, "With understanding and without."'... Ahmad was imprisoned and tortured for twenty-eight months under the Abbasid caliph al-Mu'tasim in an effort to force him to publicly espouse the [*Mu'tazila*] position that the Holy [Qur'an] was created, but the Imam bore up unflinchingly under the persecution and refused to renounce the belief of *Ahl al-Sunna* that the [Qur'an] is the uncreated word of Allah, after which Allah delivered and vindicated him. When Ahmad died in 241/855, he was accompanied to his resting place by a funeral procession of eight hundred thousand men and sixty thousand women, marking the departure of the last of the four great *mujtahid* Imams of Islam."

Ibn al-Jawzi narrates with his chain from Bilal al-Khawass that the latter met al-Khidr and asked him: "What do you say of al-Shafi'i?" He replied: "He is one of the Pillar-Saints *(al-awtâd)*." "And Ahmad ibn Hanbal?" He said: "He is a *Siddîq*."[63] When he was advised to invoke

---

[63]Ibn al-Jawzi, *Manaqib al-Imam Ahmad* (p. 144).

against his oppressors Ahmad replied: "He is not a *sâbir* who invokes against his oppressor."[64]

---

[64]Ibn Abi Ya'la, *Tabaqat al-Hanabila* (2:289); al-Dhahabi, *Siyar A'lam al-Nubala'* (9:434-547 #1876), *Tadhkira al-Huffaz* (2:431 #438).

Ibn 'Abd al-Salam:
The Belief of the People of Truth
(AL-MULHA FÎ I'TIQÂD AHL AL-HAQQ)[65]

Exordium

In the Name of Allah, the All-Beneficent, the Most Merciful. All praise belongs to Allah the Owner of power and majesty, infinite might and perfection, favor and munificence, the One, and One Alone, Unique, Everlasting, Who neither begets nor is begotten, and unto Whom nothing compares.

What Allah Is Not

He is not a body endowed with form. He is not a substance confined by boundary or measurement. He resembles nothing and nothing resembles Him. Directions and sides do not encompass Him. Neither the earths nor the heavens contain Him.

His Preternity (Beginninglessness)

He was before He brought place and time into existence, and He is now as He ever was.[66]

---

[65]In al-'Izz ibn 'Abd al-Salam, *Rasa'il al-Tawhid* (p. 11-27) and Ibn al-Subki, *Tabaqat al-Shafi'iyya al-Kubra* (8:219-229).

[66]Cf. hadith of the Prophet ﷺ: *kâna allâhu wa lâ shay'a ma'ahu / ghayruhu / qablahu* – "Allah existed and nothing existed together with Him / other than Him / before Him." Narrated from Burayda by al-Hakim in *al-Mustadrak* (2:341), who declared it sound *(sahih)* – al-Dhahabi concurred – and from 'Imran ibn Husayn by Bukhari, Ibn Hibban with two sound chains in his *Sahih* (14:7 #6140, 14:11 #6142), and Ibn Abi Shayba in his *Musannaf*. See Appendix, "Allah is now as He ever was."

His Acts

He created creatures as well as their actions. He decreed the extent of their sustenance and the term of their lives. Every benefit from Him is from His favor, and every punishment is from His justice. ❪He will not be questioned as to what He does, but they will be questioned.❫ (21:23)

He established Himself over the glorious Throne in the way that He says and the meaning He intends, "established" in a manner transcending contact *(mumâssa)*, settledness *(istiqrâr)*, fixity *(tamakkun)*, indwelling *(hulûl)*, or movement *(intiqâl)*.[67]

Exalted is Allah the Greatest, the Most High, far above the claims of the people of error and misguidance! Never can the Throne carry Him, rather the Throne and the Throne-Bearers are carried up by the subtlety of His infinite might, and all are powerless *(maqhûrûn)* in His grasp.[68]

---

[67]See the appendix entitled *"Istiwâ' is a Divine Act"* in our translation of Bayhaqi's *al-Asma' wa al-Sifat*, published separately. Note that the "Salafis" deny most of the above: "The 'Salafis' and Ibn Taymiyya assert that settledness takes place over the Throne.... Ibn Taymiyya strenuously asserts that Allah descends, and can be above *(fawq)* and below *(taht)* 'without how'.... and that the school of the *Salaf* is the affirmation of everything that the Qur'an stated concerning aboveness *(fawqiyya)*, belowness *(tahtiyya)*, and establishment over the Throne." Abu Zahra, *al-Madhahib al-Islamiyya* (p. 320-322). Ibn Rushd in *Sharh al-'Utbiyya* stated that Malik's position is: "The Throne is not Allah's location of settledness *(mawdi' istiqrâr Allâh)*." As quoted in *Fath al-Bari* (1959 ed. 7:124 #3592).

[68]"We assert that Allah established Himself over the throne without His need *(hâja)* nor settlement *(istiqrâr)* upon it, for He it is Who preserves the Throne and other than it without needing any of them." Abu Hanifa, *Wasiyya al-Imam al-A'zam ila Abi 'Amr 'Uthman al-Batti* (p. 10). "Allah established Himself over the Throne in the sense that He said and the meaning that He wills, with an establishment that transcends touch, settlement, location, immanence, and displacement. The Throne does not carry him, rather the Throne and its carriers are carried by the subtleness of His power, subdued under His grip." Al-Ash'ari, *al-Ibana 'an Usul al-Diyana*, Mahmud ed. (p. 21); Sabbagh ed. (p. 35), as translated in Shaykh Hisham Kabbani's *Islamic Beliefs and Doctrine According to Ahl al-Sunna* (p. 169). "The carrier of the Throne and of its carriers is in reality Allah Himself." Abu Sulayman al-Khattabi (d. 386) as quoted in Bayhaqi, *al-Asma' wa al-Sifat* (al-Hashidi ed. 2:279-280).

His Knowledge

He encompasses all things with His knowledge. He knows the number of all things hat exist. He is well aware of the buried recesses of the hearts and the movements of thought.

His Seven Main Attributes[69]

He is living *(hayy)*, willing *(murîd)*, hearing *(samî')*, seeing *(basîr)*, knowing *('alîm)*, mighty *(qadîr)*, and speaking *(mutakallim)* with a beginningless *(qadîm)* pre-existent *(azalî)* speech consisting neither in letter *(harf)* nor voice *(sawt)*.[70]

---

[69]These are the *sifât ma'nawiyya* or "Attributes pertaining to forms." Al-Sanusi said: (*Hashiya al-Bajuri* p. 61-75): "Necessary for Him are seven Attributes, named *sifât al-ma'âni* ["Attributes of Forms"], which are power *(al-qudra)*, will *(al-irâda)*, knowledge *('ilm)*, life *(al-hayât)*, hearing *(al-sam')*, sight *(al-basar)*, speech *(al-kalâm)*. Next there are seven attributes called *sifât ma'nawiyya* ["Attributes Pertaining to Forms"], inseparable from the previous seven, namely: His being powerful, willing, knowing, living, hearing, seeing, and speaking." The *Mu'tazila* denied the "Attributes of Forms" but accepted the "Attributes Pertaining to Forms." Their reasoning for doing so was that Allah is perfect and complete in Himself and therefore not in need, for example, of an attribute of knowledge by which He knows, for He is All-Knowing in His essence. They claimed that the logical consequence of the "Attributes of Forms" was "multiplicity of beginningless entities" *(ta'addud al-qudamâ')*. This reasoning was refuted by the entirety of *Ahl al-Sunna* scholars. See al-Buti, *Kubra al-Yaqinat al-Kawniyya* (p. 119 n.).

[70]Al-Qurtubi (d. 671) stated in his *Tafsir* or commentary of Qur'an entitled *al-Jami' li Ahkam al-Qur'an*, concerning the verse ❨The month of Ramadan in which was revealed the Qur'an❩ (2:185) which contains the phrase: ❨Allah desires ease for you...❩: "The verse indicates that Allah is willing *(murîd)* with a beginningless, pre-existent will which stands in addition to His Entity. This is the school *(madhhab)* of *Ahl al-Sunna*. Likewise, He is knowledgeable with true knowledge, able with true ability, living with true life, hearing with true hearing, seeing with true sight, and speaking with true speech. All these are pre-existent existential meanings superadded to the Essence *(ma'âni wujûdiyya azaliyya zâ'ida 'alâ al-dhât)*." See Appendix, "Allah's Names Are Ordained and Non-Inferable." Concerning the verse ❨And Our word unto a thing, when We intend it, is only that We say unto it: Be! and it is❩ (16:40) al-Qurtubi says: "There is evidence in this verse that Allah Almighty wills all phenomena – good and bad, beneficent and harmful."

His Speech Does Not Materialize

It must never be imagined that His speech turns to ink on tablets and pages or into a design *(shakl)* made visible to the eyes and the pupils, as claimed by the people of gross anthropomorphism *(al-hashw)* and dissimulation *(al-nifâq)*. Rather, the act of writing is of the doing of human beings, and their acts must never be imagined to be without beginning.

Note that it is obligatory to hold the tablets and pages in the utmost respect as they point to Allah's Entity *(dhât)*, just as it is obligatory to hold His Names in the utmost respect because they point to His Entity. It is a right due to every thing that points to Allah or relates to Him that it be held in great reverence and that its sanctity *(hurma)* be kept. Hence it is obligatory to revere the Ka'ba, the Prophets, the devout *(al-'ubbâd)*, and the scholars of knowledge *(al-'ulamâ')*.

> *I pass by the houses – Layla's houses –*
> *And I kiss this wall, and that wall;*
> *It is not the love of houses that has obsessed my heart*
> *But the love of those who have dwelled in them.*[71]

Because of something similar to this we kiss the Black Stone, and it is forbidden for someone in a state of minor impurity to touch a volume of the Qur'an: whether it be the lines of its text, or its blank margins, or its leather binding, or the pouch in which it is kept.[72]

Therefore, woe to him who asserts that Allah's preternal speech is in any way formed of the utterances of human beings, or of designs penned in ink!

---

[71] *Diwan Majnun Layla*, p. 170.

[72] In our time a certain scholar has claimed that it was permissible for menstruating women and those in a state of major defilement *(junub)* to recite, touch, and carry the Qur'an. This was refuted by Shaykh Hasan 'Ali al-Saqqaf in a book entitled *I'lam al-Kha'id bi Tahrim al-Qur'an 'ala al-Junub wa al-Ha'id* ("The Appraisal of the Investigator Into the Interdiction of the Qur'an to Those in a State of Major Defilement and Women in Their Menses").

His Ninety-Nine Names And The Enduring Good Deeds

The belief of al-Ash'ari – may Allah have mercy on him – consists in what the Ninety-Nine Names of Allah have indicated, by which He has named Himself in His Book and in the Sunna[73] of Allah's Messenger.

Allah's Names, in turn, are incorporated *(mundarija)* into four phrases. These phrases are the Enduring Good Deeds.[74]

Subhân Allâh

The first phrase is *subhân Allâh* or "Glorified is Allah!" The meaning of these two words in the language of the Arabs is transcendence *(al-tanzîh)* and negation *(al-salb)*. The phrase consists in the negation of all blemish or imperfection from Allah's Essence and Attributes. All the divine Names that denote negation are incorporated into this phrase. For example, *al-Quddûs*, "the Most Holy," which means most pure of all blemish, and *al-Salâm*, "Security," as He is secure from any defect.

Al-Hamdu Lillâh

The second phrase is *al-hamdu lillâh* or "All praise belongs to Allah!" It consists in affirming all kinds of perfection for His Essence and Attributes. Accordingly, all of His Names that form an affirmation, such as *al-'Alîm*, the Omniscient; *al-Qadîr*, the Omnipotent; *al-Samî'*, the All-Hearing; and *al-Basîr*, the All-Seeing – all these names are incorporated into this second phrase.

We have thus negated, by saying *subhân Allâh*, any conceivable blemish or defect, and we have affirmed, by saying *al-hamdu lillâh*, every manner of perfection *(kamâl)* ever known, and every trait of majesty *(jalâl)* ever seen.

---

[73]See Appendix, "The Meaning of *Sunna*."
[74]See Appendix, "The Enduring Good Deeds."

Allâhu Akbar

After what we have negated and affirmed, there still remains much of immense importance which is invisible and unknowable to us. This matter is realized in broad terms by our saying: *Allâhu akbar*, "Allah is greater!" – and this is the third phrase – in the sense that He is far greater yet than all we have negated and affirmed.

This is the meaning of the Prophet's ﷺ saying: "I cannot sufficiently extol Your praise! Verily, You are just as You have glorified Yourself."[75] Accordingly, all of His Names which form praise beyond what can be known and seen, such as *al-A'lâ*, "the Highest," and *al-Muta'âl*, "the Sublime" – these names are incorporated into our saying *Allâhu akbar*.

Lâ Ilâha Illallâh

Since there exists a being whose standing is such as we have mentioned, we now negate all possibility that there exist any other similar being or rival. We accomplish this by saying *lâ ilâha illallâh*, "There is no God except Allah": this is the fourth phrase.

Indeed, Godhead *(al-ulûhiyya)* attaches by right to deservingness of worship *(istihqâq al-'ubûdiyya)*, while none deserves worship except He Who possesses all the attributes we have mentioned. It follows that those of His Names that comprise all [His qualities] in a broad sense, such as *al-Wâhid*, "the One"; *al-Ahad*, "the One Alone"; *Dhu al-jalâl wa al-ikrâm*, "The Owner of Majesty and Munificence" – all these are incorporated into our saying: *lâ ilâha illallâh*.

Allah deserves to be worshipped precisely because it is obligatory for Him to possess all the different attributes of majesty and perfection which no-one can describe nor count:

---

[75]Narrated from 'A'isha and 'Ali in the Nine Books [al-Bukhari's *Sahih*, Muslim's *Sahih*, the four *Sunan* of al-Tirmidhi, Abu Dawud, al-Nasa'i, and Ibn Majah, the two *Musnad*s of Ahmad and al-Darimi's, and Malik's *Muwatta'*] except Bukhari and Darimi.

The wonders of your beauty do not come to an end,
Just like the sea; therefore extol it without restraint!

Glorified is He for His magnificent rank and sovereignty! ⟨**All that are in the heavens and the earth entreat Him**⟩ (55:29) due to their utter dependence on Him. ⟨**Every day He exercises universal power**⟩ (*ibid.*), for He is able to so. To Him belong all creation, commandment, sovereignty, and dominion, while creatures are powerless in His grasp: ⟨**And the heavens are rolled in His right hand**⟩ (39:67), ⟨**He punishes whom He will and He shows mercy unto whom He will, and unto Him you will be turned**⟩ (29:22). Therefore, glorified is He Who pre-exists all in His Essence and Attributes, the Reviver of the dead Who brings the remains back together, Who knows all that was and all that shall be.

The All-Inclusiveness Of *Al-Hamdu Lillâh*

The Enduring Good Deeds could easily be incorporated into a single phrase out of the four as a general heading, and that is *al-hamdu lillâh*. As 'Ali ibn Abi Talib ⁕ said: "If I wished to load a camel with [books explaining] *al-hamdu lillâh*, I could easily do so."

Indeed, glorification is praise, and praise consists in affirming perfection *(ithbât al-kamâl)* at one time, and negating imperfection *(salb al-naqs)* at another; now declaring impotence to comprehend, and now affirming that He is alone in owning all perfection. Being alone in owning all perfection is among the highest levels that command eulogy and denote perfection *(min a'la marâtib al-madh wa al-kamâl)*, and so this phrase comprises all that we have mentioned about the Enduring Good Deeds. For the definite article in the phrase [literally, "All *the* praise belongs to Allah"] signifies the comprehensive inclusion of the genus of eulogy and praise – the known as well as the unknown. Nor can any facet of praise be found not to apply to what we have mentioned. Nor is anyone deserving of divinity *(al-ilâhiyya)* except He Who possesses all the attributes which we have established.

39

The Well-Defined And Universal Doctrine

This is the belief to which none fails to subscribe: neither angel brought near, nor prophet-messenger, nor anyone in the different religious communities *(milal)* except those whom Allah has abandoned so that they follow their lusts and disobey their Lord. Such people are engulfed in base physicality, thrown out of doors, and far gone from that Exalted Presence. It is the lot of whoever was prevented *(hujiba)* in this life from hallowing Him and knowing Him, to be prevented in the next life from receiving His munificence and seeing Him.

> *Consent to the absentee's absence:*
> *Such is an offense that carries its own punishment.*

The foregoing forms the general principles of al-Ash'ari's doctrine – may Allah have mercy on him – as well as those of the *Salaf* or Predecessors[76]and the People of the Path and the Truth.[77] It stands in relation to its own detailed elucidation like a drop of water in relation to a surging ocean:

> *You have appeared and no longer remain hidden from anyone*
> *Except the blind who are oblivious to the moon.*

The Anthropomorphists

The gross anthropomorphists *(al-Hashwiyya)* who liken Allah to creation *(al-mushabbiha)* are of two types: the first make no attempt to hide their anthropomorphism. **〈And they think that they have something to**

---

[76]"The established technical definition of the term *salaf* is: the first three centuries in the age of this Muslim Community, the Community of our Master Muhammad, upon him blessings and peace. This is derived from his saying according to the narration of the Two Shaykhs [Bukhari and Muslim] from 'Abd Allah ibn Mas'ud: 'The best of people are my century, then those that follow them, then those that follow the latter. After that there will come people who will be eager to commit perjury when bearing witness.'" Al-Buti, *al-Salafiyya*, Introduction.

[77]"The People of the Path and the Truth" refers to *Ahl al-Sunna* in general – as in the title – and is sometimes used in the restricted sense to mean the Sufis.

stand upon. No, indeed! They are but liars.〉 (58:18) The second type camouflage themselves with the school of the *Salaf*, hoping thereby to gain something from ill-gotten property, if only scraps to take with them.

> *They make a show of piety before people*
> *While going around looking for cash.*[78]

〈They wish to gain your confidence with that of their people.〉 (4:91)

The Belief Of The *Salaf*

The school of the Predecessors is but the upholding of Allah's oneness *(al-tawhid)* and of His transcendence *(al-tanzih)*, without ascribing a body to Him *(al-tajsim)* nor likening Him to creation *(al-tashbih)*. Likewise, all the innovators claim that they follow the school of the Predecessors, just as the poet said:

> *Each one proclaims his kinship to Layla*
> *But Layla does not confirm it for any of them.*[79]

How can it be foisted upon the *Salaf* that they believed in ascribing a body to Allah and likening Him to creation, or that they kept quiet when innovations appeared, so thereby going against Allah's order 〈And cover not truth with falsehood, nor conceal the truth knowingly〉 (2:42), His saying 〈And remember when Allah took a covenant from the People of the Scripture, to make it known and clear to mankind and not to hide it〉 (3:187), and His saying 〈That you may explain clearly to mankind what has been revealed for them〉 (16:44)?

The Scholars' Duty Is Patterned After That Of Prophets

The scholars of knowledge are the inheritors of the Prophets.[80] It is obligatory for them to communicate and explain whatever is obligatory for

---

[78]Mahmud al-Warraq (d. ~230), cited in *al-'Uqd al-Farid* (3:216) and *al-Kashkul* (2:216).
[79]*Diwan al-Sababa* 3.
[80]See Appendix, "The Scholars are the Inheritors of Prophets."

Prophets to communicate and explain. Allah said: ⟨**Let there arise out of you a nation who invite to goodness, and enjoin right conduct and forbid indecency.**⟩ (3:104) Among the foulest indecencies are to ascribe a body to Allah and to liken Him to creation; and of the highest good is the upholding of Allah's oneness and transcendence.

The Jihad of the *Salaf* Against Innovators

The Predecessors were silent only before innovations appeared. Thereafter – this I swear by the Lord of **the heaven which gives the returning rain and the earth which splits open with vegetation!** (86:11-12) – they sprung into action and went to work against the innovations that appeared. They repressed them with lasting efficiency and deterred their proponents with a terrible swift sword. They refuted the proponents of absolute free will *(al-Qadariyya)*, the followers of Jahm ibn Safwan *(al-Jahmiyya)*, the proponents of determinism or fatalism *(al-Jabriyya)*, and other innovators. They ⟨**struggled in His cause as one ought to struggle.**⟩ (23:78)

The Duty Of Jihad Against Anthropomorphists

Struggle for Allah *(al-jihâd)* is of two types. One consists in striking the enemy with disputation and demonstration, the other in striking him with sword-blows and spears. Now, what on earth is the difference between confronting the *Hashwiyya* in disputation and confronting any other innovators?[81] Unless it were for some wickedness buried deep inside the hearts, and aberrant belief hidden within – [they would not object]! ⟨**They seek to hide from men and seek not to hide from Allah; but He is with them when by night they hold discourse displeasing unto Him.**⟩ (4:108) Should one of them be asked about something related to gross anthropomorphism he promptly orders silence concerning it, whereas if he is asked about other than anthropomorphism among the innovations – at that time he answers truthfully. If his inner disposition *(bâtinuhu)* did not harbor notions of

---

[81]This question is still unanswered today by those who object to confronting certain grievous heresies on the grounds that "we should be united." The author's intent is to bring to light their hidden agreement with the deviations which they are unwilling to denounce.

ascribing a body to Allah and likening Him to creation, he would certainly have answered by upholding Allah's oneness and declaring His transcendence.

From its inception until now, that particular sect of innovators ⟨**have been laid upon with shame wherever they are found**⟩ (3:112). ⟨**As often as they light a fire for war, Allah extinguishes it. Their effort is for corruption in the land, and Allah loves not corrupters.**⟩ (5:64) No sooner does an opportunity loom for them on the horizon but they jump to it, nor a chance for causing confusion *(fitna)* but they pounce on it.

Ahmad Ibn Hanbal's Innocence Of Their Heresies

Ahmad ibn Hanbal and the illustrious ones of his companions, as well as the rest of the learned scholars of the Predecessors are completely innocent before Allah of what has been attributed to them and invented in their name.[82] How can anyone believe that Ahmad ibn Hanbal and others of the scholars of knowledge held that Allah's preternal quality is intrinsically the very same as the pronunciation of the reciters and the ink of the scribes *(wasf Allâh al-qadîm bi dhâtihi huwa 'ayn lafz al-lâfizîn wa midâd al-kâtibîn)*![83] – when Allah's quality is beginningless, while those utterances *(alfâz)* are originated in time *(hâditha)*, as reason dictates and transmitted evidence explicitly states?

---

[82]Ibn al-Jawzi wrote in the introduction of his *Daf' Shubah al-Tashbih*: "I have advised both follower and leader in those terms: Colleagues! You are adherents and followers of our *madhhab*. Your greatest Imam is Ahmad ibn Hanbal, may Allah have mercy on him, who said, under the lash of the ordeal: 'How can I say what was never said?' Therefore, beware of innovating in his *madhhab* what is not from him!. . . Do not introduce into the *madhhab* of this man of the *Salaf*, Ahmad Ibn Hanbal, what his thought does not contain." Similarly Ibn 'Asakir narrated in his *Tabyin* (Saqqa ed. p. 164-165) that the hadith master Ibn Shahin al-Hanbali (d. 385) said: "Two righteous men have been afflicted due to evil people: Ja'far ibn Muhammad and Ahmad ibn Hanbal." Ibn al-Salah (d. 643) said: "Two imams have been afflicted because of their followers although they are innocent of them: Ahmad ibn Hanbal was tried with the anthropomorphists *(al-mujassima)*, and Ja'far al-Sadiq with the [Shi'i] Rejectionists *(al-Râfida)*." Quoted by Ibn al-Subki in his *Qa'ida* (p. 43), also found in his *Tabaqat al-Shafi'iyya al-Kubra* (2:17).
[83]See Appendix, "The Controversy Over the Pronunciation of the Qur'an" and al-Bayhaqi's documentation in our translation of *al-Asma' wa al-Sifat*, published separately.

Proofs Against The Preternality Of Recitation And Writing

Allah has declared the contingent nature *(huduth)* [of recitation and writing] in three passages of His Book. The first passage is His saying: ⟨**Never comes there unto them a new reminder *(dhikr)* from their Lord**⟩ (21:2). He has referred to what was coming to them as "new" *(muhdath)*. Therefore, whoever claims that it is beginningless has rebutted Allah ﷻ.[84]

Yes, this "new" is a sign *(dalil)* pointing to the beginningless, just as if we should write the exalted Name of Allah on a piece of paper: the preternal Lord would not thereby become indwelt or incarnate *(hallan)* in that paper. Similarly, if the beginningless quality is written down some-where, that written quality does not become indwelt where the writing took place.

The second passage is Allah's saying: ⟨**But nay! I swear by all that you see and all that you see not that it is indeed the speech of an illus-trious messenger.**⟩ (69:38-40) The messenger's speech is an attribute of his, and the quality of this contingent *(hadith)* is itself a contingent which points to the preternal speech *(yadullu 'ala al-kalam al-qadim)*. And whoever claims that the messenger's speech is beginningless has rebutted the Lord of the worlds.

Allah did not content Himself to merely declare the above but He swore to it with a most perfect oath and said: ⟨**But nay! I swear by all that you see and all that you see not.**⟩ Into this oath are incorporated His Essence and Attributes, and His creation besides.

The third passage is His saying: ⟨**But nay! I swear by the planets, the stars which rise and set, and the close of night, and the breath of morning, that this is in truth the word of an honored messenger.**⟩ (81:15-19)

---

[84]Imam Ahmad said of this verse: "It is possible that 'new' refers to the bringing down to us of the reminder, not to the reminder itself, and it is possible that the reminder be other than the Qur'an, such as the Prophet's ﷺ reminder and his admonishing them." Related by al-Bayhaqi in *al-Asma' wa al-Sifat* (al-Kawthari ed. p. 235; al-Hashidi ed. 1:572-573 #499) and Ibn Kathir in his *al-Bidaya wa al-Nihaya* (10:361). See Appendix, "The Controversy over the Pronunciation of the Qur'an" (p. 71).

Proofs Against Those Who Confuse Letter And Voice

One wonders at those who say: "The Qur'an is a combination of letter and voice" *(al-Qur'ân murakkabun min harfin wa sawt)* and then claim that all that is found in the volume of Qur'an *(al-mushaf)* when there is not, in the volume, other than the letter alone *(harf mujarrad)*, without voice. There is not in it any letter formed of voice. For the letter which is uttered *(al-harf al-lafzî)* is not the same as the written character *(al-shakl al-kitâbî)*. For that reason one perceives by ear the letter which is uttered, without seeing it, and one observes by eyesight the written character, without hearing it with the ears. May Allah not increase among the Muslims the number of the people of innovation and passion, misguidance and seduction!

Proofs Against Those Who Claim The *Mushaf* Is Preternal

As for those who say that the preternal divine quality is indwelt in the volume of Qur'an: they are compelled to conclude, if the volume of Qur'an is destroyed by fire, that Allah's preternal quality was burnt – most exalted is He high above what they say! It is a characteristic of what is beginningless not to be subject to change nor annihilation, for these certainly negate beginninglessness.

If they should claim that the Qur'an is written in the volume of Qur'an without indwelling in it, as al-Ash'ari said, then why do they curse al-Ash'ari – may Allah have mercy on him?[85] If they say other than that, then

---

[85]Ibn 'Asakir wrote in his *Tabyin* (Saqqa ed. p. 151): "The *Mu'tazila* said: 'Allah's speech is created, invented, and brought into being.' The *Hashwiyya* who attribute a body to Allah said: 'The alphabetical characters *(al-hurûf al-muqatta'a)*, the materials on which they are written, the colors in which they are written, and all that is between the two covers [of the volumes of Qur'an] is beginningless and preternal *(qadima azaliyya)*.' Al-Ash'ari took a middle road between them and said: 'The Qur'an is Allah's beginningless speech unchanged, uncreated, not of recent origin in time, nor brought into being. As for the alphabetical characters, the materials, the colors, the voices, the elements that are subject to limitations *(al-mahdûdât)*, and all that is subject to modality *(al-mukayyafât)* in the world – all this is created, brought into being, and invented.'"

45

❲See how they invent lies about Allah! That of itself is flagrant sin.❳ (4:50) ❲And on the Day of Resurrection you will see those who lied concerning Allah with their faces blackened. Is not the home of the scorners in hell?❳ (39:60)

As for Allah's saying: ❲That this is indeed a noble Qur'an in a Book kept hidden❳ (56:77-78), the imams of the Arabic language agree that there is definitely an ellipsis *(kalima mahdhûfa)* in His saying: ❲in a Book kept hidden❳: and it is obligatory to understand this ellipsis to mean: "written in a Book kept hidden." This is due to the reasons we have mentioned above, and in accordance to the criteria of reason *(al-'aql)* which testifies to divine oneness and the veracity of the Prophetic Message.

Proofs Against Those Who Reject Reason

Reason is the indispensable condition of legal responsibility *(manât al-taklîf)* according to the consensus of Muslims. However, reason was not adduced as a proof for preternality *(lam yustadall bi al-'aql 'alâ al-qidam)*: it is sufficient that it witnesses to it. Now they do not listen to its testimony, although the divine Law has long declared reason an upright witness *(al-shar' qad 'addala al-'aql)*, accepting its testimony, and has even adduced it as a proof in certain points of its Book. Examples are the inference of [the logical truth of] revival *(al-i'âda)* from [the known fact] of origination *(al-inshâ')*; or Allah's saying: ❲If there were, in the heavens and the earth, other gods besides Allah, there would have been confusion in both!❳ (21:22); or His saying: ❲Have they not considered the dominion *(malakût)* of the heavens and the earth, and what things Allah has created?❳ (7:185)

Miserable indeed is the failure of him who rejects a witness whom Allah has accepted, and invalidates a proof Allah has produced! For they refer themselves [only] to what was textually transmitted *(al-manqûl)*.[86] Because of that, we have cited only textually transmitted proofs, and we have kept securely hidden those based on reason: if we need them we can produce them, otherwise we can leave them until we do.

---

[86]See Appendix, "The Literalist Invalidation of Reason."

More Proofs Against The Preternality Of Recitation

A group-transmitted *(mashhûr)* hadith states: "Whoever recites the Qur'an and pronounces it clearly and distinctly *(a'rabahu)* receives ten blessings for each letter, and whoever recites it without pronouncing it clearly and distinctly receives one blessing for each letter."[87] However, what is beginningless cannot be marred by faulty expression *(al-lahn)* nor made perfect by means of clear and distinct pronunciation. And Allah said: **(You will be requited nothing other than what you have done.)** (37:39) Therefore, if His Prophet informed us that we would be rewarded for the recitation of the Qur'an he indicated thereby that such recitation is one of our actions – and our actions are by no means without beginning.

Allah's Naming Of The Recitation *Qur'ân*

The Qur'an and the Sunna were brought to the people in a context of utter ignorance and in the midst of simple minds and dull wits. Indeed, the word *qur'ân* applies, both in the divine Law and in language, to the beginningless object of description *(al-wasf al-qadîm)*; but it also applies to the contingent recitation *(al-qirâ'a al-hâditha)*. Allah said: **(Upon Us rest the putting together thereof and its *qur'ân*.)** (75:17) That is: its recitation.[88]

---

[87]This hadith is weak in its attribution to the Prophet ﷺ, as indicated by the author in his unattributive way of citing it, in accordance with the requirements of the Law when citing a weak hadith. Various forms of the narration are related from the Prophet ﷺ through at least five Companions – hence the nomenclature of *mashhûr* – but with weak or very weak chains, by al-Bayhaqi in *Shu'ab al-Iman* (5:241 #2096-2097), Ibn 'Adi in *al-Kamil fi al-Du'afa'* (7:2506), and al-Tabarani as stated by al-Haythami in the book of the Merits of the Qur'an in *Majma' al-Zawa'id*. Of note is the following saying of 'Umar: "Recite the Qur'an and do not leave out its clear and distinct pronunciation." Something close to it is also related from Ibn Mas'ud, both narrated by Ibn Aby Shayba in his *Musannaf* (1:158, 2:160). There is a sound narration from Ibn Mas'ud narrated by al-Tirmidhi, who graded it *hasan sahîh gharîb* ("authentic, narrated by only one Companion"), whereby the Prophet ﷺ said: "Whoever reads one letter of the Qur'an has performed a good deed, for which he receives ten the like thereof. I do not say that 'A. L. M.' (2:1) are a letter but 'A.' is a letter, 'L.' is a letter, and 'M.' is a letter."

[88]Al-Bukhari narrated in the first book of his *Sahih* (Book of Revelation) as well as Muslim in his *Sahih* (Book of Prayer, chapter entitled "Listening to the Recitation"):

For the act of recitation *(al-qirâ'a)* is different from what is being read *(al-maqrû')*: the act of recitation is of recent origin in time while what is being recited is beginningless. Similarly, when we remember or mention Allah, our remembrance is of recent origin while what is remembered is beginningless.

The foregoing is but a glimpse of the school of al-Ash'ari on the topic.

> *If Hadhâmi speaks, believe her.*
> *Verily the truth is what Hadhâmi spoke!* [89]

The Duty To Speak Out Against Anthropomorphists

There is too much to be said on the topic. If it were not incumbent upon the scholars to strengthen the Religion and undermine innovators, and if

---

From Ibn 'Abbas concerning the saying of the Exalted: ❪**Do not move your tongue with it in order to hasten it.**❫ (75:16) He said: "Allah's Messenger ﷺ experienced a certain difficulty in the process of revelation. He was of those who would move their lips [i.e. mnemonically, along with hearing recitation]. And I shall move my lips for you in the way Allah's Messenger ﷺ used to move them."

"Then Allah sent down: '**Do not move your tongue with it in order to hasten it.** [i.e. its memorization] **Its gathering and recitation rest upon us.**'" (75:16-17) Ibn 'Abbas said: "That is: its gathering in your breast and subsequent recitation."

'**And when We recite it, follow its recital.**' (75:18) Ibn 'Abbas said: "That is: listen to it and keep silent."

'**Then verily upon Us rests its exposition.**' (75:19) Ibn 'Abbas said: "That is: Upon Us rests its recitation by yourself." [Shaykh Mustafa Dib al-Bugha in his edition of *al-Tajrid al-Sarih* elaborated it to mean: the permanency of your memorization of it leading to its appearance on your tongue, also explained as the detailing of its generalities, the elaboration of its complexities, the exposition of what is in it concerning the permitted and the forbidden, and other than that.]

"After this, when Jibril came to him the Prophet ﷺ would listen, and after Jibril left the Prophet ﷺ would recite it in the manner Jibril had recited it."

[89]Lujaym ibn Sa'b or Wasim ibn Tariq, as quoted in *Lisan al-'Arab* in the entries *h-dh-m* and *r-q-sh*, also *Mughni al-Labib* (#404), *Shudhur al-Dhahab* (38:95), *Awdah al-Masalik* (1:131 #482), Ibn 'Aqil's *Tafsir* (1:85 #16), etc. This verse is a *locus classicus (shâhid)* of Arabic grammar to illustrate the dialect of the Hijaz concerning the syntagm *fa'âl*. See Ibn Hisham al-Ansari's (d. 761) *Qatr al-Nada*, chapter on *Hadhâm*.

the gross anthropomorphists had not unleashed their tongues in our time to commit calumnies against those who uphold Allah's oneness, and to spread contempt against the words of those who declare Allah's transcendence – otherwise I would not have spoken at length on a topic such as this, which is clear as day.

However, Allah has ordered us to struggle in the cause of His Religion. The only difference is that the scholar's weapons are his knowledge and his tongue, while the king's weapons are his swords and spears. Just as it is not allowed for kings to put down their weapons in the face of the atheists *(al-mulhidin)* and the Christians *(al-mushrikîn)*,[90] similarly, it is not allowed for scholars to still their tongues in the face of the heretics *(al-zâ'ighîn)* and the innovators *(al-mubtadi'în)*.

Whoever struggles with all his strength for Allah's sake so as to bring up high Allah's Religion, is going to be worthy of Allah's watchful protection, empowered with His invincible strength, defended with His support, and protected from the entire host of creation. **《And if Allah willed He could have punished them (Himself), but (thus it is ordained) that He may try some of you by means of others.》** (47:4)

Those who declare Allah's transcendence and His oneness have given and continue to give the same answers for all the world to see, at every celebration and in every place of assembly. They declare it aloud in the schools and in the mosques. The innovation of the *Hashwiyya*, however, has been kept hidden and concealed in secrecy. They have been unable to bring it out into the open, but they have instilled it to the ignorant masses. They are only beginning to bring it out into the open in our time.

Therefore we ask Allah to hasten the ruin of that innovation as is His custom, and to let its humiliation come to pass as has been His way in the past, and according to the path of those who uphold Allah's transcendence and oneness, on which the Followers *(al-Khalaf)* and the Predecessors *(al-Salaf)* have both proceeded. May Allah be well pleased with all of them.

---

[90]The author means the Mongols and the Franks who were attacking al-Sham at the time.

They Attack Al-Ash'ari for Attributing Causality to Allah

It is a wonder that they blame al-Ash'ari because he said: "Bread does not satiate, water does not quench thirst, fire does not burn [in themselves]"! For this discourse Allah Himself has revealed – in its meaning – in his Book. Indeed, satiation, quenching, and combustion are phenomena which Allah alone creates, since bread does not create satiation, nor does water create quenching, nor does fire create combustion, although they are causes for such results. But the Creator is Himself the Causator *(al-Musabbib)*, not the causes.[91]

This is just as Allah said: ❨**You threw not when you did throw, but Allah threw.**❩ (8:17) He denied that His Prophet was the creator of the throw, although he was its cause. Allah also said: ❨**And that it is He Who makes laugh, and makes weep, and that it is He Who gives death and gives life.**❩ (54:43-44) Thus He dissociated making-laugh, making-weep, the giving of death and of life from their respective causes, attributing all to Himself.

Similarly, al-Ash'ari dissociated satiation, quenching, and combustion from their causes, attributing them all to the Creator Who said: ❨**Such is Allah, your Lord. There is no God save Him, the Creator of all things.**❩ (6:102) ❨**Is there any creator other than Allah?**❩ (35:3) ❨**Nay, but**

---

[91]See Ibn Khafif's *'Aqida* §41 ("Things do not act of their own nature..."), published separately. Cf. al-Zahawi in *al-Fajr al-Sadiq*: "Food does not sate, nor does water quench thirst, nor does medicine heal. But the One who is the real Satisfier of our hunger, the Quencher of our thirst and the Healer of our ills is Allah alone. The food, the water, the medicine are only the proximate or secondary causes which custom has established on the surface of things by our mind's regular association of them with certain concomitant events." As translated in *The Doctrine of Ahl al-Sunna Versus the "Salafi" Movement* (p. 86). A man asked al-Tustari: "What is sustenance?" He said: "Perpetual *dhikr*." The man said: "I was not asking about that, but about what sustains one." He replied: "O man! Things are sustained by nothing but Allah." The man said: "I did not mean that, I asked you about what is indispensible!" He replied: "Young man, Allah is indispensible." Abu Nu'aym, *Hilya* (10:218 #15022). This is the consensus of *Ahl al-Sunna*, as opposed to the Shi'a, the *Mu'tazila*, and the philosophers such as al-Farabi and Ibn Rushd. The latter three groups subscribed to Aristotelian causality *(al-'illa al-aristiyya)* i.e. the belief that causes are given a degree of inherent causality. Ibn Taymiyya was attacked for endorsing this belief in his *al-Radd 'ala al-Mantiqiyyin* ("Against Logicians"). Cf. al-Buti, *al-Salafiyya* (p. 173).

they denied what they could not comprehend and whereof the interpretation had not yet come unto them.❭ (10:39) ❬Did you deny My signs when you could not compass them in knowledge, or what was it you did?❭ (27:84)

> *How many do reprove a truthful word*
> *When it is they who suffer from deficient understanding!*[92]

Therefore, glory to Him Who has approved of some whom He brought nearer to Him, and shown wrath to others whom He kept far from Him. ❬He will not be questioned as to what He does, but they will be questioned.❭ (21:23)

Truth And Right Are Dearer Than Life

It is incumbent on every scholar of knowledge, when he sees truth brought low and right undermined, to muster every strength of his in order to assist truth and right. He must consider himself more deserving of humiliation and incapacitation than truth and right. If he strengthens the truth and brings up high the right, let him but seek their shade, and content himself with droplets of whatever [gain] may come from elsewhere.

> *A little from you benefits me, although*
> *The little that comes from you cannot be called little.*

To risk one's life in the cause of strengthening the Religion is licit. Thus it is permitted for heroic individuals among the Muslims to plunge into the battle-ranks of the disbelievers. Similarly, to incur danger in the act of commanding good and forbidding evil, aiding to uphold the bases of the Religion through proofs and evidences, is licit. Whoever fears for his life is no longer obligated but merely encouraged to do it. As for those who say that exposing one's life to danger is impermissible, they have gone far from truth and left what is right.

---

[92]Al-Mutanabbi, *Diwan* (4:246). Compare with Imam Taqi al-Din Ibn al-Subki's (d. 756) description of a major anti-Ash'ari scholar as "one whose learning exceeded his intelligence" in his *al-Rasa'il al-Subkiyya* (p. 151-152).

Allah Prefers Whoever Prefers Him

In sum, whoever prefers Allah above himself, Allah will prefer him. Whoever seeks Allah's approval with what angers people, Allah shall be well-pleased with him and shall make people pleased with him also. But whoever seeks people's approval with what displeases Allah, Allah shall be angry with him and shall make people angry with him also. There is sufficiency, in Allah's approval, from that of everybody else.

So long as You are sweet, let all life be bitter.
So long as You are pleased, let all creatures be wroth.[93]

And

All things lost can be replaced
But Allah has not, if you lose Him, any replacement.

The Prophet ﷺ said: "Keep Allah well and He shall keep you well. Keep Allah well and you shall find Him in front of you" *(tajidhu amâmak).*[94]

---

[93] Abu Firas al-Hamadani, *Diwan* (1:24).

[94] Some versions other than Tirmidhi's mention the wording cited here, while Tirmidhi's version mentions: "and you shall find Him facing you" *(tajidhu tujâhak).* Narrated from Ibn 'Abbas as part of a longer hadith by Ahmad in his *Musnad* with a sound chain as stated by Shaykh Ahmad Shakir in his edition (3:194 #2669); Tirmidhi in his *Sunan* with two similar chains, and he graded it *hasan sahih*; Bayhaqi in *al-Asma' wa al-Sifat* (al-Hashidi ed. 1:188 #126) – as part of his explanation of Allah's attributes *al-Dârr al-Nâfi'* ("The Bringer of Harm and of Benefit") – with a sound chain as stated by its editor 'Abd Allah al-Hashidi; and Abu Ya'la al-Musili in his *Musnad* (4:430 #2556). Ibn Rajab al-Hanbali cites it in his *Jami' al-'Ulum wa al-Hikam* ("The Compendium of the Sciences and the Words of Wisdom") and declares it authentic (1:359-361). Imam al-Nawawi cites it in his *Riyad al-Salihin* and as the nineteenth of his "Forty Hadiths." The complete narration states: "I was [riding] behind the Prophet ﷺ one day and he said to me: 'O my boy! I shall teach you certain words. Keep Allah, and He will keep you. Keep Allah, and you shall find Him facing you. If you ask for something, ask Allah. If you ask for help, ask it from Allah. Know with certainty that if the entire Community gathered together to support you, they can benefit you nothing but what Allah has foreordained for you; and if they gathered together in order to harm you, they can harm you in nothing but what Allah has foreordained against you. The quills have been raised and the records are dry.'" Imam Ahmad added in his narration: "Make yourself known to Allah in the time of prosperity and He shall know you in the time of affliction. Know that patience in the

It has also been mentioned in the hadith: "Remind Allah of yourselves! In truth, Allah gives His servant the same status in His presence as that which His servant gives Him in himself."[95] Accordingly one of the eminent authorities said: "Whoever wants to know in what regard Allah holds him, let him see in what regard he holds Allah."

Final Supplication

O Allah! Grant victory to the Truth! Bring up high the right! Confirm for this Community right conduct, whereby Your Friends shall be firmly established and Your enemies brought low, obedience to You put into practice, and rebellion against you firmly kept in check!

And all praise belongs to Allah Who is my support and upon Whom I rely. He is sufficient for me. Most excellent is He in Whom I trust! And may Allah send blessings and peace, honor and favor, praise and munificence on our Master Muhammad, and upon his Family and all his Companions. *Amin. Amin.*

---

face of what you hate is an immense good, that help lies with patience, deliverance with trial, and with hardship goes ease."
[95]Narrated from Jabir ibn 'Abd Allah by al-Hakim in the *Mustadrak* (1:494), al-Bazzar in his *Musnad*, al-Tabarani in *al-Awsat*, al-Bayhaqi in *Shu'ab al-Iman*, Abu Ya'la in his *Musnad*, Ibn Shahin, and Ibn 'Asakir, all with chains containing 'Umar ibn 'Abd Allah Mawla Ghufra, declared trustworthy by Ahmad, Muhammad ibn Sa'd, and al-Bazzar, but weak by Yahya ibn Ma'in al-Nasa'i, Ibn Hibban, al-Dhahabi, and Ibn Hajar as stated in *Mizan al-I'tidal* (3:210 #6155) and *Taqrib al-Tahdhib* (p. 414 #4934). The narration is therefore weak, and the author accordingly referred to it in non-attributive, passive mode.

Appendix 1

The Title *Shaykh al-Islâm*
(by SHAMS AL-DIN AL-SAKHAWI)[96]

"*Shaykh al-Islam*," as inferred from its use as a term among the authorities, is a title attributed to the follower of the book of Allah and the example of His messenger 𐀃 , who possesses the knowledge of the principles of the Science (of Religion), who has plunged deep into the different views of the scholars, has become able to extract the legal evidences from the texts, and has understood the rational and the transmitted proofs at a satisfactory level.

At times, this title is given to those who have attained the level of friendship with Allah *(wilâya)*, and from whom people derive blessings both when they are alive and when they are dead. Similarly, whoever has tread the true path of the People of Islam and has come out unscathed from the folly and ignorance of youth; and whoever has become a living apparatus for others in solving difficulties or winning a struggle, and a refuge in every difficulty: these are the meanings of the word as used by the general public.

At times, this title is also given to those who get old in the fold of Islam and become outstanding among their peers for long life, entering into the meaning of the hadith "There will be a light for those who grow old in the fold of Islam."[97]

---

[96] Al-Sakhawi, *al-Jawahir wa al-Durar*, p. 14-23.

[97] Narrated from 'Amr ibn Abasa by al-Tirmidhi *(hasan sahih gharib)*, al-Nasa'i, and Ahmad; from Ka'b ibn Murra by al-Tirmidhi *(hasan)*, al-Nasa'i, Ahmad, and al-Daraqutni in his *Sunan*; from 'Abd Allah ibn 'Amr by Abu Dawud; from 'Umar by Ibn Hibban with a strong chain (*Sahih* 7:251 #2983), al-Tabarani in *al-Kabir* (1:58), Ibn Rahuyah, and Abu Nu'aym in *Ma'rifa al-Sahaba*; from Mu'adh ibn Jabal by al-Tabarani in *al-Kabir*; from Abu Nujayh al-Sulami by Ibn Hibban with a sound chain (*Sahih* 7:252 #2984), al-Bayhaqi in the *Sunan* (9:161), and, as part of a longer hadith, by Ahmad with a sound chain; from Abu al-Darda' by Abu al-Shaykh; from Jabir by Ibn 'Asakir; from Abu Hurayra by al-Quda'i in *Musnad al-Shihab* (p. 457); from Fadala ibn 'Ubayd by al-Tabarani in *al-Kabir* (18:782-783), and Ahmad and al-Bazzar in their *Musnad*s; and from Umm Sulaym by al-Hakim in *al-Kuna*; also from 'Amr ibn 'Abasa but as part of a longer hadith, by Ahmad with a sound chain, and al-Bayhhaqi in the *Sunan* (9:272).

This title was not common among the earlier generations after the two Shaykhs, al-Siddiq and al-Faruq, and we know that 'Ali applied it to them ☬. Al-Muhibb al-Tabari (d. 694) related in his book *al-Riyad al-Nadira* ["The Resplendant Groves"], without providing a chain of authorities, that Anas ☬ said that a man came to 'Ali ibn Abi Talib ☬ and said: "O Commander of the Faithful, I heard you saying on the pulpit 'O Allah, help me as you helped the rightly-guided and enlightened caliphs.' Who are they?" Anas said: Tears welled in 'Ali's eyes and began to pour down, then he replied: "Abu Bakr and 'Umar, may Allah be well pleased with them, the two leaders of rightful guidance and the two shaykhs of Islam, the two men of Quraysh, the two who are followed after the Messenger of Allah ☬. Whoever follows these two gains respect; whoever lives up to the legacy of these two is guided to a straight path; whoever sticks with these two is from Allah's party, and Allah's party – these are the successful."[98]

Al-Dhahabi reported in *al-Kashif* on the authority of Ibn al-Mubarak (d. 118) – mark him, O Reader, as one who was a *Shaykh al-Islam*: "The only one to carry the title *Shaykh al-Islam* is Abu Bakr al-Siddiq ☬, who preserved the *zakat* and fought against the apostates. Know this very well." The report ends here.

Isma'il al-Harawi (d. 481) came to be known with this title. His full name was 'Abdullah ibn Muhammad al-Ansari, a Hanbali scholar and the author of *Manazil al-Sa'irin* and *Dhamm al-Kalam*.[99] Abu 'Ali Hassan ibn Said al-Mani'i al-Shafi'i and Abu al-Hassan al-'Ukkari were also known with this title. Ibn al-Sam'ani said about the latter that he was called *Shaykh al-Islam*. He also was a Shafi'i.

---

[98]Muhibb al-Din al-Tabari, *al-Riyad al-Nadira* (1:379 #276). Al-Zamakhshari, *Mukhtasar al-Muwafaqa* f° 23.

[99]Al-Dhahabi frequently identifies him as *Shaykh al-Islam* in his works. He also authored *al-Faruq fi al-Sifat* in refutation – like *Dhamm al-Kalam* – of the Ash'aris, in which al-Dhahabi in *Mukhtasar al-'Uluw* (p. 278 #339) quotes him as saying: "Allah is in the seventh heaven *(fi al-sama' al-sabi'a)* over the Throne *('ala al-'arsh)* Himself *(bi nafsihi)*." Al-Shakhawi further in his biography quotes Ibn Hajar as citing *Dhamm al-Kalam* as an example of bad writing, forbidding his students to read it. Al-Harawi's statement that Allah is in *(fi)* as well as over *('ala)* the seventh heaven is related by al-Dhahabi in *Mukhtasar al-'Uluw* (p. 151 #150).

Among the scholars of the Hanafi school the following carried this title:

- Abu Saʿid al-Khalil ibn Ahmad ibn Muhammad ibn al-Khalil al-Sajzi, who died after 370;
- Abu al-Qasim Yunus ibn Tahir ibn Muhammad ibn Yunus al-Basri – Ibn Mandah mentions him – who died in 411;
- The judge Abu al-Hasan Ali ibn al-Husayn ibn Muhammad al-Sughdi who died in 461 – also called *Rukn al-Islam* (Pillar of Islam);
- Abu Nasr Ahmad ibn Muhammad ibn Saʿid al-Saʿidi. Al-Dhahabi said about him: "He is one of those who are called *Shaykh al-Islam.*" He died in 482;
- Ali ibn Muhammad ibn Ismail ibn Ali al-Isbijabi, who died in 535;
- His student, the author of *al-Hidaya*, Burhan al-Din Ali ibn Abu Bakr ʿAbd al-Jalil al-Farghani, who died in 593;
- Muhammad ibn Muhammad ibn Muhammad al-Halabi [d. 817];
- al-ʿImad Masʿud ibn Shaybah ibn al-Husayn al-Sindi;
- Abu Saʿd al-Mutahhar ibn Sulayman al-Zanjani;
- Sadid ibn Muhammad al-Hannati.

The master Abu ʿUthman Ismaʿil ibn ʿAbd al-Rahman ibn Ahmad al-Sabuni al-Shafiʿi was also known by this title. Ibn al-Samʿani gave it to him in al-Dhayl. Also known by this title was Taj al-Din al-Firkah, who was a Shafiʿi. Ibn Daqiq al-ʿId (d. 702) gave this title to his master Ibn ʿAbd al-Salam. He said: He is *Shaykh al-Islam.* Also known by this title were Abu al-Faraj ibn ʿUmar the Hanbali, the first who undertook the jurisdiction for the Hanbalis (in Mecca), Ibn Daqiq al-ʿId himself, Ibn Taymiyya – Abu al-Hajjaj al-Mizzi (d. 742) did not give this title to anyone else among his contemporaries besides him – Ibn Abi ʿUmar, Taqi al-Din al-Subki, in whose time and in whose son's time the use of this title increased, especially in Damascus. Later, Siraj al-Din al-Bulqini (Ibn Hajar's shaykh) was given this title. I read in Ibn ʿAmmar's own hand that it was used exclusively for him...

Since the beginning of the eigth century innumerable people have been given this title, to the extent that even the chief judges came to be called with it even if they lacked the knowledge and the age. Indeed, ignorant writers and other than they took to attributing individuals all manners of qualities which nowadays exist only among selected persons. Those who

confirm them in this abuse are the strangest of all. Verily we belong to Allah and to Him do we return.

Ibn Hajar, may Allah have mercy on him, entirely merits being called with this title because he had most of the qualities that are mentioned above, and when that title was used by the authorities in his time he was meant and no-one else. Even if he was not an authority in everything, in the field of the hadith of the Prophet 鬣 he was, beyond question, *Shaykh al-Islam*. Ahmad ibn Hanbal, whose piety is beyond question, called Abu al-Walid al-Tayalisi and Ahmad ibn Yunus *Shaykh al-Islam* although they had only the knowledge of hadith, whereas Ibn Hajar's authority was not limited to this one field only. May Allah have mercy on them and us![100]

---

[100]Ibn Hajar himself applied the title of *Shaykh al-Islam* to his teacher, the hadith master Zayn al-Din al-'Iraqi, unless he named someone else. Cf. "Our shaykh, *Shaykh al-Islam*, said..." *Fath al-Bari* (1:18 #1; 1:27 #3; 1:33 #7; 1:192 #97; 1:458; 3:361 #1425; 8:223 #4278 etc.), but "Our shaykh, *Shaykh al-Islam* al-Bulqini said..." *Ibid.* (1:22 #2; 13:547 #7124; cf. 1:45). Like al-Sakhawi, al-Suyuti applies the title to Ibn Hajar, while both al-Haytami and al-Sha'rani apply it to their shaykh, Zakariyya al-Ansari.

Appendix 2

"Allah Is Now As He Ever Was"

The saying "Allah existed eternally without a place, and He is now as He ever was" is related – without chain – from ʿAli ibn Abi Talib ﷺ.[101] Ibn ʿAtaʾ Allah al-Sakandari (d. 709) cites it as one of his *Hikam* (#34).

Imam Abu Hanifa (d. 150) said: "Had He been in a place and needing to sit and rest before creating the Throne, then the question ʿWhere was Allah?' would have applied to Him, which is impossible."[102]

The position of Imam Abu al-Hasan al-Ashʿari is thus summed up by Abu al-Qasim ibn ʿAsakir:

> The *Najjariyya* said: 'The Creator is in every place without indwelling *(hulûl)* nor direction *(jiha).*' The *Hashwiyya* and the *mushabbiha* said: 'The Creator took His place *(hâllun)* on the Throne, the Throne is His location *(makân)*, and He is sitting on top of it.' Al-Ashʿari took a middle ground between the two and said: ʿAllah existed when there was no place; then He created the Throne and the Footstool *(al-ʿarsh wa al-kursi)* without ever being in need of place, and He is, after creating place, exactly as He was before creating it.'[103]

This is the position of al-Ashʿari also as given by Ibn Jahbal al-Kilabi (d. 733): "The words of the Shaykh [Abu al-Hasan al-Ashʿari] concerning direction are: ʿAllah was when there was no place, then He created the Throne and the Footstool, without ever needing place, and He is, after creating place, exactly as He was before creating it.'"[104] Ibn Jahbal also says in his *Refutation of Ibn Taymiyya*:

---

[101]As cited by ʿAbd al-Qahir al-Baghdadi (d. 429) in his *al-Farq Bayn al-Firaq* (p. 256).
[102]Abu Hanifa, *Wasiyya al-Imam al-Aʿzam* (p. 10).
[103]In the *Tabyin* (Saqqa ed. p. 150).
[104]In *Tabaqat al-Shafiʿiyya al-Kubra* (9:79).

22. We say: Our doctrine is that Allah is pre-eternal without beginning *(qadim azali)*. He does not resemble anything nor does anything resemble Him. He has no direction nor place. He is not subject to time nor duration. Neither "where" *(ayn)* nor "at" *(hayth)* applies to Him. He shall be seen, but not as part of an encounter, nor in the sense of an encounter *(yurâ lâ 'an muqâbala wa lâ 'alâ muqâbala)*. He was when there was no place, He created place and time, and He is now as He ever was. This is the *madhhab* of *Ahl al-Sunna* and the doctrine of the shaykhs of the [Sufi] Path – may Allah be well-pleased with them.[105]

30. Muhammad ibn Mahbub, Abu 'Uthman al-Maghribi's servant, said: "Abu 'Uthman said to me one day: 'O Muhammad! If someone asked you: Where is the One you worship, what would you answer?' I said: 'I would answer: He is where He never ceased to be.' He said: 'What if he asked: Where was He in pre-eternity?' I said: 'I would answer: Where He is now. That is: He was when there was no place, and He is now as He ever was.' Abu 'Uthman was pleased with my answer. He took off his shirt and gave it to me."[106]

Sulayman ibn 'Abd Allah ibn Muhammad ibn 'Abd al-Wahhab (d. 1817CE), the Wahhabi founder's grandson, said:

Whoever believes or says: Allah is in person *(bi dhâtihi)* in every place, or in one place: he is a disbeliever. It is obligatory to declare that Allah is separate *(bâ'in)* from His creation, established over His throne without modality or likeness or examplarity. Allah was and there was no place, then He created place and He is exalted as He was before He created place.[107]

---

[105] In *Tabaqat al-Shafi'iyya al-Kubra* (9:41).
[106] In *Tabaqat al-Shafi'iyya al-Kubra* (9:43).
[107] In his *al-Tawdih 'an Tawhid al-Khallaq fi Jawab Ahl al-'Iraq* (1319/1901, p. 34, and new ed. al-Riyad: Dar Tibah, 1984).

Appendix 3

Allah's Names And Attributes Are *Tawqîfiyya* : Ordained And Non-Inferable

Imam al-Ash'ari said: "My method in the application of Allah's Names is [based on] permission in the Law, without [reference to] lexical analogy."[108]

Ibn Khafif said in his *al-'Aqida al-Sahiha*:

> 23. The divine Attributes are obtained only from the transmitted sources, that is, either what Allah said of Himself, or what the Prophet 🕮 said of Him, or what the Muslims concur about in relation to a given attribute.

> 24. The divine Names are not obtained by making up surnames *(talqiban)* nor by analogical derivation *(qiyâsan)*.

> 25. Neither the Names nor the Attributes are created.

Like *murîd* and *dâ'im, qadim* which we translated as "beginningless" and "preternal," and *azalî* which we translated as "pre-existent," *mutakallim* is among the rare attributes ascribed to Allah by scholars such as al-Bayhaqi in *al-Asma' wa al-Sifat*, al-Qurtubi in his *Tafsir*, as well as earlier scholars, from inference rather than an explicit textual precedent in the Qur'an and Sunna, although this may not be true of *al-Qadim*, which is cited in the texts.

Al-Bayhaqi wrote the following in his introduction to the "chapters which affirm the attribute of purpose *(al-mashî'a)* and will *(al-irâda)* for Allah" in his *al-Asma' wa al-Sifat* (1:349):

> The teacher Abu Ishaq [al-Isfarayini] (d. 418) used to say: 'Among the Names of the attributes of the Essence *(asâmi sifât al-dhât)* are those which pertain to will, such as: the Merciful *(al-Rahmân)*, that is, He Who wills the sustenance of all that is alive in

---

[108] In Ibn al-Subki's *Tabaqat al-Shafi'iyya al-Kubra* (3:358).

the abode of trial and tribulation; the Beneficent *(al-Rahim)*, He Who
wills the lavishing of grace on the dwellers of Paradise; the Forgiving
(al-Ghaffar), He Who wills the cancellation of punishment
established as deserved; the Cherisher *(al-Wadud)*, He Who wills
goodness for those who are His Friends; the Clement *(al-'Afuw)*, He
Who wills facilitation for those who are His Knowers; the
Compassionate *(al-Ra'uf)*, He Who wills kindliness for all His
creatures; the Patient *(al-Sabur)*, He Who wills the reprieve of
punishment; the Gentle *(al-Halim)*, He Who wills the cancellation of
punishment from the root of the offense; the Generous *(al-Karim)*,
He Who wills the abundance of resources for those in need; the
Righteous *(al-Barr)*, He Who wills the strengthening of those who
are His Friends.'

The scholars said that Allah's Names and Attributes are "ordained
and non-inferable" *(tawqifiyya)*. Some, like Ibn Hazm, have criticized, for
example, the inference of the definite name *al-Qadim* – which lacks an
explicit basis in the texts – from the agreed-upon attribute of *qadim*, since the
meaning of *al-Qadim* is adequately provided by *al-Awwal* ("The First") in the
verse: "He is the First and the Last" (57:3).[109]

Ibrahim al-Laqqani (d. 1041) states in *Jawhara al-Tawhid* (v. 39):

It was decided that Allah's Names are ordained and so are
His Attributes, therefore memorize the transmitted evidence.

Shaykh Muhammad Muhyi al-Din 'Abd al-Hamid in his supercom-
mentary on 'Abd al-Salam al-Laqqani's (d. 1078) explanation of the above
entitled *Ithaf al-Murid bi Jawhara al-Tawhid* said:

The meaning of the Names and Attributes being ordained and
non-inferable is that it is not permitted for anyone to assert an
attribute or a name for Allah except if there is an explicit text *(nass)*
from Allah or His Prophet allowing the use of such a name or
attribute. . . . Even if the name or attribute point to pure perfection,
Ahl al-Sunna hold that it is not permitted to apply either to Allah
without a specific permission. The 'Isolationists' or Rationalists
(Mu'tazila) considered that it is permitted to assert [a name or

---

[109]See Ibn Abi al-'Izz's commentary on the *'Aqida Tahawiyya* (p. 114-115).

attribute] the meaning of which describes Allah, provided it does not suggest any imperfection. [Among *Ahl al-Sunna*] al-Qadi Abu Bakr Ibn al-Baqillani (d. 403) [a foremost exponent of al-Ash'ari and a Maliki jurist] inclined towards the latter, while Imam al-Haramayn [Abu al-Ma'ali 'Abd al-Malik al-Juwayni] (d. 478) did not decide one way or the other, and [his student] al-Ghazali (d. 505) differentiated the name from the attribute. He considered it allowed to use an [inferred] attribute in the definite mode [e.g. *al-qidam*] – as the attribute is what indicates a meaning in addition to the Essence – and impermissible to use a name in the definite mode, as the name is what indicates the Essence itself. . . . Therefore the scholars differed in only point: and that is, when there is no explicit text from the Lawgiver on applying or prohibiting a certain Name or Attribute which, in addition, points to pure perfection.[110]

Bayhaqi in *al-Asma' wa al-Sifat* (1:115) related the following from al-Halimi: "Offensive things, since they do not befit Him, cannot serve to derive His names from their names. Only applicable to Him are the names that can be derived *(tashtaqq)* from attributes denoting perfection."

About *al-Qadim* al-Jurjani says in his *Ta'rifat*:

> *Al-qadim* applies to what exists without its existence proceeding from another than itself; this is the "*qadim* in essence." It also applies to what exists and whose existence is not preceded by non-existence; this is the "*qadim* in time"... Every "*qadim* in essence" is also "*qadim* in time," but not every "*qadim* in time" is "*qadim* in essence."... It is also said: The "*qadim*" is that for which there is no beginning and no end.

Al-Qadim is mentioned in the hadith as one of the ninety-nine names of Allah: "... *al-Qarib* ("The Near"), *al-Raqib* ("The Watchful"), *al-Fattah* ("The Opener"), *al-Tawwab* ("The Relenting One"), *al-Qadim*, *al-Witr* ("The Unpaired"), *al-Fatir* ("The Creator"), *al-Razzaq* ("The Provider"), *al-'Allam* ("The Knower"), etc."[111]

---

[110]Muhammad Muhyi al-Din 'Abd al-Hamid, *al-Nizam al-Farid* (Aleppo: Dar al-Falah, 1990) p. 126-127.
[111]Narrated by al-Hakim, Abu al-Shaykh and Ibn Mardawayh in their Commentary on the Qur'an, and Abu Nu'aym in his *al-Asma' al-Husna*, through Abu Hurayra.

The Prophet 🕮 used "Allah, *al-Qadîm*" in his supplications.[112]

Al-Sakhawi quotes verses from the hadith master of Damascus Ibn Nasir al-Din where Allah is referred to as *al-Qadîm*:

> *Allah has brought back to life the Prophet's mother and father*
> *So that they would believe in him, as a kind gift from Him.*[113]
> *Verily the Pre-eternal One (al-Qadîm) is able to do this,*
> *Even if the hadith that states it is weak.*

The Prophet 🕮 said this supplication upon entering the mosque:

> *a'ûdhu billâh al-'azim wa bi wajhihi al-karim*
> *wa sultânihi al-qadim min al-shaytân al-rajîm*

I seek refuge in Allah the Exalted and in His Gracious Countenance and in His Ancient Sovereignty from the accursed satan.[114]

Qadîm as an adjective is also used for created objects, as is clear from the Qur'an: ❨**You are in your old aberration**❩ (12:95), ❨**They say: This is an ancient lie**❩ (46:11), and the advice given by the Companion Abu 'Ubayda ibn al-Jarrah:

> *Bâdiru al-sayyi'ât al-qadîmât bi al-hasanât al-hadîthât*
> Requite old evils with new good deeds.

---

[112]Cf. hadith in Ibn Majah (Book of *Du'a*, Chapter 10).
[113]The narrations on this issue were collected by al-Sha'rani in the chapter on the Prophet's 🕮 parents in his book *al-Mizan al-Kubra*. See also al-Suyuti's epistle *Masalik al-Hunafa' fi Abaway al-Mustafa* 🕮, translated in Shaykh Hisham Kabbani's *Encyclopedia of Islamic Doctrine*.
[114]Narrated from 'Abd Allah ibn 'Amr ibn al-'As by Abu Dawud. A fair *(hasan)* hadith according to al-Nawawi, al-Suyuti, and al-Munawi.

Appendix 4

The Meaning Of *Sunna*

The Arabic word *sunna* lexically means "road" or "practice." In the language of the Prophet 豢 and the Companions it denotes the whole of licit practices followed in the Religion, particularly the untainted *(hanif)* path of the Prophets, whether pertaining to belief, religious and social practice, or ethics generally speaking.

In its technical sense *sunna* has three meanings. In hadith terminology it denotes any saying *(qawl)*, action *(fiʻl)*, approval *(taqrir)*, or attribute *(sifa)*, whether physical *(khilqiyya)* or moral *(khuluqiyya)* ascribed to *(udifa ila)* the Prophet 豢, whether before or after the beginning of his prophethood. This meaning is used in contradistinction to the Qurʼan in expressions such as "Qurʼan and Sunna" and applies in the usage of hadith scholars.

In the terminology of *fiqh* or jurisprudence, *sunna* denotes whatever is firmly established *(thabata)* as required *(matlūb)* in the Religion on the basis of a legal proof *(dalil sharʻi)* but without being obligatory, the continued abandonment of which constitutes disregard *(istikhfāf)* of the Religion – also sin *(ithm)* according to some jurists – and incurs blame *(lawm, ʻitāb, tadlil)* – also punishment *(ʻuqūba)* according to some jurists. This meaning is used in contradistinction to the other four of the five legal categories for human actions – *fard* (obligatory), *sunna*, *mubāh* (indifferent), *makrūh* (disliked), *harām* (prohibited) – and applies in the usage of jurists from the second Hijri century onwards. However, the jurists have stressed that the basis for all acts of worship categorized as *sunna* is "obligatoriness" not "permissiveness" *(al-asl fi al-sunna al-wujūb lā al-ibāha)*.[115] *Sunna* is thus defined by them as the strongest of the following near-synonymous categories:

> "praiseworthy" *(mandūb)*
> "desirable" *(mustahabb)*

---

[115]This is contrary to the misconception of latter-day *fiqh* instructors who say: "Such-and-such is *merely* a Sunna."

"voluntary" *(tatawwu')*
"refinement" *(adab)*
"obedience" *(ta'a)*
"supererogatory" *(nafl)*
"drawing near" *(qurba)*
"recommended" *(raghiba, murghab fih)*
"excellent" *(hasan)*
"excellence" *(ihsan)*
"meritorious" *(fadila)*
"best" *(afdal)*.

It is antonymous with "innovation" *(bid'a)*, as in the expression "People of the Sunna" or Sunnis *(Ahl al-Sunna)*.

In the terminology of *usul al-fiqh* or principles of jurisprudence, *sunna* denotes any saying *(qawl)*, action *(fi'l)*, or approval *(taqrir)* related from *(nuqila 'an)* the Prophet ﷺ or issued from him *(sadara 'anh)* other than the Qur'an.[116]

---

[116]See Shaykh 'Abd al-Fattah Abu Ghudda's *Lamahat Min Tarikh al-Sunna wa 'Ulum al-Hadith* ("Glimpses from the History of the Sunna and the Hadith Sciences") p. 11-14 and his *al-Sunna al-Nabawiyya wa Bayan Madluliha al-Shar'i* ("The Prophetic Sunna and the Exposition of Its Meaning in Islamic Law") p. 7-24; and 'Abd al-Ghani 'Abd al-Khaliq's *Hujjiyya al-Sunna* ("The Probativeness of the Sunna," Herndon, VA: 1993) p. 51-84.

Appendix 5

The Enduring Good Deeds

❨Wealth and children are an ornament of life of the world. But the enduring good deeds are better in your Lord's sight for reward, and better in respect of hope.❩ (18:46) ❨Allah increases in right guidance those who walk aright, and the enduring good deeds are better in your Lord's sight for reward, and better for resort.❩ (19:76) Asked what are the Enduring Good Deeds the Prophet 🕮 replied: "They are *lā ilāha illallāh, subhān Allāh, al-hamdu lillāh, allāhu akbar*, and *lā hawla wa lā quwwata illā billāh.*"[117]

He also said: "[These] four are the best of all discourses, and it is indifferent whatever you begin with: *subhān Allāh wa al-hamdu lillāh wa lā ilāha illallāh wallāhu akbar.*"[118] It is also narrated as follows: "There is no speech dearer to Allah than *al-hamdu lillāh wa subhān Allāh wallāhu akbar wa lā ilāha illallāh*: they are only four words, so I do not find them too much to say, and it is indifferent whichever you begin with."[119]

He said: "To say *subhān Allāh* and *al-hamdu lillāh* and *lā ilāha illallāh* and *Allāhu akbar* is dearer to me than everything under the sun."[120]

And he said two or three times: "Take up your shields!" They said: "O Messenger of Allah, because of an enemy that showed up presently?" He said: "No, I meant your shields from the Fire, which consist in saying: *subhān Allāh* and *al-hamdu lillāh* and *lā ilāha illallāh* and *Allāhu akbar*. In truth, those phrases shall come on the Day of Resurrection both in front of you and behind you, carrying great good. They are the Enduring Good Deeds."[121]

---

[117]Narrated from 'Uthman by Imam Ahmad with a sound chain as indicated by Shaykh Ahmad Shakir (*Musnad* 1:383 #513) and Haythami in *Majma' al-Zawa'id* (1:297).
[118]Narrated from Samura ibn Jundub by Muslim, Ahmad, and Ibn Majah.
[119]Narrated from Samura ibn Jundub by Muslim.
[120]Narrated from Abu Hurayra by Muslim and Tirmidhi, who declared it *hasan sahih.*
[121]Narrated from 'A'isha by Ibn Abi Shayba; Abu Hurayra by Tabarani in his *Saghir* and *Awsat* with a sound (*sahih*) chain, Tabari (sura 18:46), and al-Hakim who

declared it sound; and Anas by Tabarani in *al-Awsat* with a weak *(da'if)* chain. Something similar is narrated from Abu Sa'id al-Khudri by Ahmad in his *Musnad*, al-Hakim in his *Mustadrak*, and Ibn Hibban in his *Sahih*, all with weak chains, and by Tabari in his *Tafsir* with a fair *(hasan)* chain, as stated by Shaykh Shu'ayb Arna'ut in his edition of Ibn Hibban's *Sahih* (3:121 #840), although al-Haythami declared Ahmad's chain fair in *Majma' al-Zawa'id*.

Appendix 6

"The Scholars Are The Inheritors of Prophets"

The saying "The scholars of knowledge are the inheritors of Prophets"[122] mentioned by al-'Izz ibn 'Abd al-Salam is in fact part of a long hadith of the Prophet 🕌.

The hadith narrated from Abu al-Darda' by Abu Dawud in the opening of the Book of Knowledge of his *Sunan* states that Kathir ibn Qays states:

> I was sitting with Abu al-Darda' in the mosque of Damascus. A man came to him and said: "Abu al-Darda', I have come to you from the city of Allah's Messenger 🕌 for a narration which I have heard that you relate from him. I have come for no other purpose." [Abu al-Darda'] said: "I heard Allah's Messenger 🕌 say: 'If anyone travels on a road in search of knowledge, Allah will cause him to travel on one of the roads of Paradise, the angels will lower their wings from pleasure with one who seeks knowledge, and the dwellers of the heavens and the earth and the fish in the depth of the sea will ask

---

[122]Narrated from Abu al-Darda' by al-Tirmidhi, Abu Dawud, and Ibn Majah in their *Sunan*, Ahmad and al-Darimi in their *Musnads*, Ibn Hibban in his *Sahih*, and al-Bukhari in "suspended" form *(mu'allaq)*, without chain, in the Book of Knowledge of his *Sahih*, chapter entitled "Knowledge [comes] before talk and action." Ibn Hajar in *Fath al-Bari* mentions its strengthening through its many chains. It is also cited by al-Tahawi in *Mushkil al-Athar* (1:429), al-Baghawi in *Sharh al-Sunna* (1:275 #129 *gharib*), Ibn 'Abd al-Barr in *Jami' Bayan al-'Ilm* (p. 37-41), and others. It is a fair *(hasan)* hadith as stated by Shaykh Shu'ayb al-Arna'ut in his commentary on Ibn Hibban's *Sahih* (1:290) and Abu al-Ashbal al-Zuhayri in his commentary on Ibn 'Abd al-Barr's *Jami' Bayan al-'Ilm* (1:160 #169). Al-Raghib al-Asfahani (d. 425) in his *Mufradat Alfaz al-Qur'an* under the entry *w-r-th* has: "Suyuti said: 'al-Nawawi said it was weak *(da'if)* – that is: in its chain – even if it is true *(sahih)* – that is: in its meaning. Al-Mizzi said: "This hadith has been narrated through chains which give it the rank of *hasan*." It is as al-Mizzi said, and I have seen fifty chains for it, which I listed in a book.' Here end Suyuti's words." Note that the declaration of this hadith as *da'if* by al-'Ajluni in *Kashf al-Khafa'* is incorrect, while the claim of the editor of Qari's *al-Asrar al-Marfu'a* (p. 232) that al-'Iraqi declared it *sahih* in his *al-Ba'ith 'ala al-Ikhlas min Hawadith al-Qussas* (#31) seems doubtful in the light of 'Iraqi's reserve toward the hadith in the opening of his *Mughni 'an Haml al-Asfar*.

forgiveness for the learned man. The superiority of the learned man over the ordinary believer is like that of the moon on the night when it is full over the rest of the stars. The learned are the inheritors of the Prophets, and the Prophets have neither dinar nor dirham, they leave only knowledge, and he who takes it takes an abundant portion.'"

Although the portion al-'Izz ibn 'Abd al-Salam quoted is a fair narration, he did not positively attribute it to the Prophet ﷺ in keeping with his great caution when citing hadiths, and he followed Bukhari's non-attributive precedent in the *Sahih*.

Shaykh Ahmad Shakir in his notes on Ahmad's narration of this hadith in the *Musnad* (16:71 #21612) erred on three counts: by grading its chain *hasan* though it is *da'if* as cited from Ahmad; by claiming that Tirmidhi declared his own narration of the hadith *hasan* – whereas he did not, but he declared its chain disconnected *(laysa bi muttasil)*; and finally by claiming that "none of the scholars mentioned any weakening" for Ahmad's and Tirmidhi's sub-narrator Kathir ibn Qays (or Qays ibn Kathir as he is also named). Perhaps Shakir only looked up Ibn Hibban's *Thiqat* where Kathir is listed as unknown. However, both al-Daraqutni and Ibn Hajar declared him weak *(da'if)*.[123]

---

[123] As stated in Dhahabi's *Mizan al-I'tidal* (2:5 #2599, 3:409 #6947) and Ibn Hajar's *Taqrib al-Tahdhib* (p. 460 #5624).

Appendix 7

The Controversy Over The Pronunciation of the Qur'an[124]

Ahl al-Sunna agree one and all that the Qur'an is Allah's pre-existent, pre-eternal, uncreated speech. Imam Malik gave the most succint statement of this doctrine: "The Qur'an is Allah's speech, Allah's speech comes from Him, and nothing created comes from Allah."[125] Where the imams differed was over the pronunciation of the Qur'an. Some, like Bukhari, Muslim, and the entire Ash'ari school, held that the pronunciation was created, while others, like the Hanbalis (other than Imam Ahmad), insisted that the pronunciation was governed by the same belief in uncreatedness as the Qur'an itself.

It is narrated that Muhammad ibn Isma'il al-Sulami heard Imam Ahmad say: "The 'pronunciationists' – those who say that their pronunciation of the Qur'an is created – are Jahmis *(al-lafziyya jahmiyya)*. Allah said: **'Until he hears Allah's speech'** (9:6). From whom does he hear it?"[126] This is similar to the hadith master Musaddad ibn Musarhad al-Asadi's (d. 228) narration from Ahmad with a weak chain: "Whatever is in the volumes of Qur'an *(masahif)*, whatever recitation is performed by the people, whatever way it is recited, and whatever way it is described: all this is Allah's speech, uncreated. Whoever says it is created is a disbeliever in Allah Almighty; and whoever does not declare him so, is himself a disbeliever! . . . Some of the Jahmis said: 'Our pronunciation of the Qur'an is created': All these are disbelievers."[127]

Despite the apparent authenticity of their transmission, nevertheless the above relations are misleading and most likely inauthentic. Al-Bukhari

---

[124]See al-Buti, *Kubra al-Yaqinat* (p. 126-127). Also see above, Ibn 'Abd al-Salam's extensive explanations in the sections entitled "His Speech Does Not Materialize" (p. 36), "Proofs Against the Preternality of Recitation and Writing" etc. (p. 45-48).

[125]Al-Dhahabi, *Siyar* (7:416).

[126]Narrated with a chain of reliable narrators by Ibn Abi Ya'la in *Tabaqat al-Hanabila* (1:280 #388).

[127]Also in the *Tabaqat* (1:342 #494).

said in *Khalq Af'al al-'Ibad*: "As for what the two parties from the school of Ahmad have claimed as proof, each for his own position: Much of what they relate is not established as authentic."[128] Ibn al-Subki said that what was (authentically) related from Imam Ahmad is that he declared as an innovation, not disbelief, al-Karabisi's statement that one's pronunciation of the Qur'an was created *(lafzuka bihi makluq)*.[129] What reconciles the two views reported from Ahmad is that some may have given his words the most severe meaning possible, namely the sense of a *bid'a mukaffira* or innovation that constitutes disbelief. Note that it was also al-Karabisi's view that whoever contradicts his statement that one's pronunciation of the Qur'an was created commits disbelief, and so Ahmad did not contradict it, but declared it an innovation instead.

Such doctrines are largely a reaction explained by the charged climate prevalent in Ahmad's time and the sway of the *Jahmiyya* over the caliphate which culminated in the persecution of *Ahl al-Sunna* scholars. At the time of Imam Ahmad's 28-month[130] detention and lashing by the authorities he was pressed to admit to the creation of the Qur'an by the following arguments as narrated by his son Salih ibn Ahmad ibn Hanbal:

> Questioner: What do you say about the Qur'an?
>
> Ahmad: And you, what do you say about Allah's knowledge?
>
> Another questioner: Did not Allah say: ❲**Allah is the Creator of all things**❳ (13:16), and is not the Qur'an a thing?
>
> Ahmad: Allah also said: ❲**Destroying all things**❳ (46:25), then it destroyed all except whatever Allah willed.
>
> Another questioner: ❲**Never comes there unto them a new reminder from their Lord**❳ (21:2). Can something new be anything but created?
>
> Ahmad: Allah said: ❲**Sâd. By the Qur'an that contains the Reminder.**❳ (38:1) "The" reminder is the Qur'an, while the other verse does not say "the".
>
> Another questioner: But the hadith of 'Imran ibn Husayn states: "Allah created the Reminder."

---

[128] As quoted by al-Kawthari in his edition of *al-Asma' wa al-Sifat* (p. 266).

[129] Ibn al-Subki, *Tabaqat al-Shafi'iyya* (2:118-119).

[130] Shaykh Shu'ayb Arna'ut's mention of "ten years" in his introduction to *Sahih Ibn Hibban* (p. 22) is inaccurate.

Ahmad: That is not correct, several narrated it to us as: "Allah wrote the Reminder."[131]

Then they forwarded the hadith of Ibn Mas'ud: "Allah did not create a garden of Paradise nor a fire of Hell nor a heaven nor an earth more tremendous *(a'zam)* than the verse of the Throne (2:255)."[132]

Ahmad: The creating here applies to the garden, the fire, the heaven, and the earth. It does not apply to the Qur'an.

Another questioner: The narration of Khabbab states: "I admonish you to approach Allah with all that you can; but you can never approach Him with something dearer to Him than His speech."[133]

Ahmad: And that is true.[134]

The Hanbalis sometimes went too far in their reaction, as demonstrated by the boycott of Imam al-Bukhari led by the *Amir al-Mu'minin fi al-Hadith* ("Commander of the Faithful in the Science of Hadith") of Khurasan, Muhammad ibn Yahya al-Dhuhli (d. 258), whom Abu Zur'a ranked above Muslim and who once said: "I have made Ahmad ibn Hanbal an Imam in all that stands between me and my Lord."[135] Al-Dhuhli's boycott led Bukhari's ultimate expulsion from Naysabur for saying something that aroused their suspicion that he was a *Jahmi!*[136] Ibn al-Subki relates the incident and elaborates on it:

Abu Muhammad ibn 'Adi said: "Many shaykhs mentioned to me that when Muhammad ibn Isma'il (al-Bukhari) came to Naysabur and was attended by the throngs of people, some of the shaykhs

---

[131]Bukhari, *Sahih*, book of the Beginning of Creation: "Allah was when there was nothing else than Him, and His Throne was over the water, and He wrote in the Reminder *(al-dhikr)* all things, and He created the heavens and the earth."

[132]Narrated by Sa'id ibn Mansur, Ibn al-Mundhir, Ibn al-Daris, al-Tabarani, al-Harawi in his *Fada'il*, and al-Bayhaqi in *Shu'ab al-Iman*, as stated by al-Suyuti in *al-Durr al-Manthur*. Al-Tirmidhi in his *Sunan* mentions Sufyan ibn 'Uyayna's explanation whereby this is because the garden, the fire, etc. are all created as opposed to the Qur'an.

[133]Narrated by al-Hakim (2:441) who declared it sound – al-Dhahabi concurred – and by al-Bayhaqi in *al-Asma' wa al-Sifat* with two sound chains (al-Hashidi ed. 1:587-588 #513-514).

[134]Al-Dhahabi, *Siyar A'lam al-Nubala'* (9:478), Ibn al-Subki, *Tabaqat al-Shafi'iyya al-Kubra* (2:46-47).

[135]Narrated by al-Dhahabi in the *Siyar* (10:205).

[136]Cf. al-Dhahabi, *Siyar* (10:207, 10:311-316).

73

began to feel jealous of him and said to the authorities in hadith: 'Muhammad ibn Isma'il says: "The pronouncing of the Qur'an is created," so investigate him.' When the people gathered, one man got up and asked him: 'O Abu 'Abd Allah, what do you say about pronouncing the Qur'an, is it created or uncreated?' He ignored him and did not reply, so the man repeated the question, so he ignored him again, so he repeated it again, at which point Bukhari turned to him and said: 'The Qur'an is Allah's speech and is uncreated; the actions of servants are created; and investigating someone is an innovation.' At this the man cried out, there was a general uproar, the crowd dispersed, and Bukhari sat alone in his house."

Muhammad ibn Yusuf al-Farabri said: I heard Muhammad ibn Isma'il say: "As for the actions of servants, they are created: 'Ali ibn 'Abd Allah narrated to us: Marwan ibn Mu'awiya narrated to us: Abu Malik narrated to us from Rib'i from Hudhayfa who said that the Prophet ﷺ said: 'Truly, Allah makes every maker and his making.' *(innallâha yasna'u kulla sâni'in wa san'atahu.)*[137] And I heard 'Ubayd Allah ibn Sa'id say: I heard Yahya ibn Sa'id say: I can still hear our companions saying: 'Truly, the actions of servants are created.'

Al-Bukhari continued: "Their motions *(harakât)*, voices *(aswât)*, earning *(iktisâb)*, and writing *(kitâba)* are created. As for the Qur'an that is declaimed *(matluw)*, established *(muthbat)* in the volumes, inscribed *(mastûr)*, written *(maktûb)*, contained *(mû'a)* in the hearts: that is Allah's speech, uncreated. Allah said: **'But it is clear revelations in the hearts of those who have been given knowledge.'** (29:49) [Bayhaqi's narration in *al-Asma' wa al-Sifat* (2:7 #570) adds: al-Bukhari said: Ishaq ibn Ibrahim said: "As for the containers, who doubts that they are created?"]

"It is said: 'So-and-so's recitation is excellent,' and 'So-and-so's recitation is bad.' It is not said: 'His Qur'an is excellent' or 'His Qur'an is bad.' And to the servants is the recitation attributed, for the Qur'an is Allah's speech, while the recitation is the act of the servant,

---

[137]Narrated by al-Bukhari in *Khalq Af'al al-'Ibad*, al-Bayhaqi in *al-Asma' wa al-Sifat* with three sound chains and in the *Shu'ab*, and al-Hakim in *al-Mustadrak* with a sound *(sahîh)* chain as confirmed by al-Dhahabi.

and no-one can legislate concerning Allah without knowledge unlike some have claimed when they said that the Qur'an is one with our pronouncing it, that our pronouncing it is one thing together with it, that declamation *(al-tilâwa)* is itself the thing declaimed *(al-matluw)*, and recitation *(al-qirâ'a)* is itself the thing recited *(al-maqrû')*. Such a one must be told: declamation is the act of the reciter and the deed of the one declaiming."

Abu Hamid al-A'mashi said: "I saw al-Bukhari at the funeral of Sa'id ibn Marwan, at which time al-Dhuhli was asking him about the names and patronyms [of narrators] and the defects [of narrations], and al-Bukhari was going through them like an arrow. Not a month passed after that but al-Dhuhli told us: 'Whoever goes to his gathering, let him not come to ours. They wrote to us from Baghdad that he spoke about pronuncia-tion [of the Qur'an], and we ordered him to stop, which he did not, therefore do not go near him.'" It had been related from Bukhari that he had said: My pronunciation of the Qur'an is created, while al-Dhuhli had said: "Whoever claims that his pronunciation of the Qur'an is created, he is an innovator whose company must be shunned, and whoever claims that the Qur'an is created has committed disbelief."

Muhammad ibn Yahya only meant – and Allah knows best – what Ahmad ibn Hanbal meant, namely to forbid from entering into that subject. He did not mean to contradict Bukhari. If he did mean to contradict him and to claim that the pronunciation which comes out of his own created lips is preternal, that would be an enormity. One would like to believe that he meant other than that and that both he, Ahmad ibn Hanbal, and other imams only meant to prohibit people from entering into problems of *kalâm* (dialectic theology). For us, Bukhari's words are to be understood as a permission to mention *kalâm* if needed, since the use of *kalâm* out of necessity is an obligation *(wâjib)*, while keeping silence about *kalâm* in other than necessity is a *sunna*.[138]

---

[138]This position is reiterated by Ibn al-Subki's younger contemporary al-Shatibi (d. 790) in his book *al-Muwafaqat* (2:332): "Malik ibn Anas used to say: 'I detest talking about Religion, just as the people of our country [al-Madina] detest and prohibit it, in the sense of Jahm's doctrine, *qadar*, and the like. I do not like to speak except about what relates to practice. As for talk about the Religion, I prefer to keep silent about

Understand this well, and leave the rantings of historians, and ignore once and for all the distortions of the misguided who think that they are scholars of hadith and that they are standing on the Sunna when in fact they could not be further from it. How could anyone possibly think that Bukhari has anything in common with the position of the *Mu'tazila* when it has been authentically reported from him by al-Farabri and others that he said: "I consider as ignorant whoever does not declare the Jahmis to be disbelievers"? The impartial observer will not doubt that Muhammad ibn Yahya al-Dhuhli suffered from envy, from which none is safe except those who are immune to sin. Some even asked Bukhari about him and he said: "How can envy concerning learning possess Muhammad ibn Yahya, when learning is Allah's wealth which He gives whomever He pleases?"

Bukhari gave a sample of his great intelligence when in reply to Abu 'Amr al-Khaffaf who said to him: People are examining your words "My pronunciation of Qur'an is created" Bukhari said: "O Abu 'Amr, remember what I say to you: Whoever claims, among the people of Naysabur, Qamus, Rayy, Hamadhan, Baghdad, Kufa, Basra, Mecca, and Madina, that I ever said: 'My pronunciation of Qur'an is created,' he is a liar; truly I never said it. All I said is: The actions of servants are created."

Observe his words well and see how intelligent he is! Its meaning is – and Allah knows best: "I did not say that my pronunciation of Qur'an is created for to say such would constitute entering into problematics of dialectical theology and of the attributes of Allah wherein it is unfitting to enter except due to necessity; what I said is: the actions of servants are created, and it is a general foundation which exempts one from mentioning the problematics specifically. For every rational person understands that our pronunciation is part of our actions, and our actions are created, therefore our pronunciation is created."

---

it.' The Congregation of [Sunni] Muslims follow Imam Malik's position, except if one is obliged to speak. One must not remain silent if his purpose is to refute falsehood and guide people away from it, or if one fears the spread of misguidance or some similar danger."

He has made this meaning explicit in another sound narration reported from him by Hatem ibn Ahmad ibn al-Kindi who said: I heard Muslim ibn al-Hajjaj say – and he recounted the narration in which is the following: "A man stood before Bukhari and asked him about the pronunciation of Qur'an, and he replied: 'Our actions are created, and our pronunciation is part of our actions.'" The story also mentions that the people at that time differed concerning Bukhari, some saying that he had said: My pronunciation of Qur'an is created, others denying it. I say: The only ones to blame are those who indulge in discourse concerning the Qur'an.

In conclusion we repeat what we said in the biography of al-Karabisi:[139] Ahmad ibn Hanbal, and others of the masters of learning to whom Allah has granted success, forbade people to discourse concerning Qur'an although they did not differ (with Bukhari) on the question of pronunciation. This is what we believe about them with due respect for them, based on their sayings in other narrations, and in order to exonerate them from saying something which neither reason nor transmitted evidence support. Furthermore, al-Karabisi, Bukhari, and others of the imams to whom Allah has granted success have made it explicit that their pronunciation is created when they felt the necessity to make it explicit, if it is established that they actually took such an explicit position.[140] We have otherwise brought to the reader Bukhari's saying that whoever relates that he said such a thing, he has reported something false from him.

The reader may ask: If it is the truth then why did he not say it explicitly? I answer: Glory to Allah! We have told you that the gist of this matter is their insistence prohibiting discussions of dialectical theology lest such discussions take them to unseemly consequences. Not every science can be explicited, therefore remember what we impart to you and hold on to it tightly.

---

[139]See *Tabaqat al-Shafi'iyya* (2:118-120).
[140]Such as al-Harith al-Muhasibi, Muhammad ibn Nasr al-Marwazi, Muslim ibn al-Hajjaj, and Ahmad ibn Salama.

I like what Ghazali quotes in *Minhaj al-'Abidin* attributing it to a member of the Prophet's 鬱 House, Zayn al-'Abidin 'Ali ibn al-Husayn ibn 'Ali:

> *I keep the jewels of my knowledge concealed*
> *Lest the ignorant see Truth and turn away.*
> *How many an essential knowledge, if I divulged it,*
> *I would be told for it: You are of the idol-worshippers;*
> *And righteous men would deem licit my blood*
> *And think well of the ugly deed they would commit.*
> *This is what Abu al-Hasan ('Ali) had already*
> *Advised al-Husayn and, before him, al-Hasan.*[141]

The position that was finally retained by the Hanbali school on the question is less extreme, as shown by Ibn Qudama's (d. 620) statement on the subject:

Part of Allah's speech is the noble Qur'an, Allah's Book that clarifies all, His firm rope, His straight path, the revelation of the Lord of the worlds. The faithful Spirit brought it down to the heart of the master of Messengers in a clear Arabic tongue. It is revealed, not created, from Him [Allah] did it issue and to Him it shall return. It consists in precise suras, clear verses, letters and words. Whoever recites it *(qara'ahu)* and pronounces it clearly and distinctly *(a'rabahu)* shall receive ten blessings for every letter. It has a beginning and an end, sections and parts. It is recited *(matluwwun)* with the tongues, preserved in the breasts, heard with the ears, written in the volumes. It comprises the precise and the ambiguous, the abrogating and the abrogated, the specific and the general, the command and the prohibition. **'No falsehood can approach it from before or behind it: it is sent down, by One Full of Wisdom, worthy of all Praise'** (41:42). **'Say: if the whole of mankind and Jinns should assemble to produce the like of this Qur'an, they could not produce the like thereof, even if they backed up each other with help and support'** (17:88).[142]

---

[141]Ibn al-Subki, *Tabaqat al-Shafi'iyya al-Kubra* (2:228-231).
[142]Ibn Qudama, *Lam'a al-I'tiqad* (p. 17 #13).

Another authoritative statement of the Sunni doctrine on the topic is given by Taj al-Din Ibn al-Subki:

> The Qur'an itself is really written in the volumes *(al-masāhif)*, preserved in the hearts of the believers, read and recited in reality with the tongues of the reciters among the Muslims, just as Allah Almighty is really, and not metaphorically, worshipped in our mosques, known in our hearts, and mentioned with our tongues. This is clear, with Allah's grace and thanks to Him. Whoever deviates from this path is an 'isolationist' proponent of absolute free will *(qadarī mu'tazilī)*.[143]

Of note is Ibn al-Subki's sharp contradiction of the image given by Ibn Abi Ya'la of Imam Ahmad, and Ibn al-Subki's twofold denial: first, that Imam Ahmad ever considered the doctrine that pronunciation is created as disbelief; second, that he ever held that the pronunciation of the Qur'an was uncreated.[144] Al-Dhahabi's position, on the other hand, is to ascribe both views to Imam Ahmad.[145] At the same time he admits, in somewhat circuitous fashion, the difference between pronunciation *(al-talaffuz)* and its content *(al-malfūz)*, recitation *(qirā'a)* and its content *(al-maqrū')*, and the contingent *(muhdath)* nature of pronunciation, voice *(al-sawt)*, movement *(al-haraka)*, and utterance *(al-natq)*, although loath to admit frankly that they are created.[146] The only possible exception is in al-Dhahabi's notice on Al-Ash'ari's companion, the Shafi'i scholar al-Karabisi.[147] When al-Karabisi heard that Imam Ahmad had declared his statement an innovation whereby the pronunciation of the Qur'an was created, he said: "Pronunciation means other than the thing pronounced" *(talaffuzuka ya'ni ghayra al-malfūz)*. Then he said of Ahmad: "What shall we do with this boy? If we say 'created' he says *bid'a*, and if we say 'not created' he says *bid'a*." Al-Dhahabi commented: "There is no doubt that what al-Karabisi innovated and explained in the question of the pronunciation is the truth, but Imam Ahmad refused it in order to preclude the extension of the question to the Qur'an itself, since one cannot distinguish the pronunciation from the pronounced, which is Allah's speech, except in the mind."

---

[143]Ibn al-Subki, *Tabaqat al-Shafi'iyya al-Kubra* (3:418).
[144]In the *Tabaqat al-Shafi'iyya* (2:118-120).
[145]*Siyar* (9:503-505).
[146]*Siyar* (9:505).
[147]Al-Dhahabi. *Siyar* (10:81-82 #1988).

Al-Dhahabi considers that at the root of the disagreement lay a strict refusal, on the part of Imam Ahmad's circle, to countenance any concession to what they considered dialectic theology *(kalâm)* and therefore innovation. This attitude was not shared by al-Bukhari and Muslim among others:

Al-Dhuhli was fierce *(shadîd)* in his adhesion to the Sunna. He confronted Muhammad ibn Isma'il [al-Bukhari] because the latter had alluded, in his *Khalq Af'al al-'Ibad*, to the fact that the reader's utterance of the Qur'an was created. Bukhari made it understood without explicitly saying it, but he certainly made it clear. On the other hand Ahmad ibn Hanbal flatly refused to explore the question, as well as Abu Zur'a and al-Dhuhli, or indulge in the terminology of dialectic theologians *(al-mutakallimûn)*, and they did well – may Allah reward them excellently. Ibn Isma'il had to travel from Naysabur under cover, and he was pained by what Muhammad ibn Yahya [al-Dhuhli] had done to him.[148]

Among those who narrated from al-Dhuhli is Muhammad ibn Isma'il al-Bukhari [34 hadiths according to Ibn Hajar in *Tahdhib al-Tahdhib* 9:516], but he conceals his name a lot *(yudallisuhu kathiran)*. He does not name him "Muhammad ibn Yahya" but only "Muhammad," or "Muhammad ibn Khalid," or "Muhammad ibn 'Abd Allah," linking him to his great-grandfather [and grandfather respectively] and obscuring his name because of the incident that took place between them.[149]

Al-Hakim [narrated with his chains]: Muhammad ibn Yahya [al-Dhuhli] said: "This Bukhari has openly subscribed to the doctrine of 'pronunciationists' *(al-lafziyya)*, and for me those are worse than the *Jahmiyya*." ... Ahmad ibn Salama visited Bukhari and told him: "O Abu 'Abd Allah, this is a respected man [i.e. al-Dhuhli] in Khurasan, especially in this town [Naysabur], and he has thundered with this speech until none of us can say anything to him about it, so what do you think we should do?" Bukhari grasped his beard then he said: ⟨I confide my cause unto Allah. Lo! Allah is Seer of His slaves.⟩ (40:44) He continued: "O Allah! You know that I did not

---

[148] Al-Dhahabi, *Siyar* (10:207).
[149] Al-Dhahabi, *Siyar* (10:201).

want for one moment to settle in Naysabur out of arrogance, nor in quest of leadership, but only because my soul would not let me return to my own country [Bukhara] because of my opponents; and now this man intends harm for me out of jealousy, only because of what Allah gave me and for no other reason." Then he said to me: "O Ahmad, tomorrow I shall leave and you will be rid of his talk which I caused." . . . Muhammad ibn Ya'qub the hadith master said: "When al-Bukhari settled in Naysabur Muslim ibn al-Hajjaj took to visiting him frequently. When the affair of the pronunciation of Qur'an took place between al-Bukhari and [al-Dhuhli] and the latter roused people against him and forbade them to visit him, most people stopped visiting him, but not Muslim.[150] Then al-Dhuhli said: 'Anyone that subscribes to the pronunciation [being created], it is not permitted for them to attend our gathering.' Whereupon Muslim placed a cloak on top of his turban, stood up in front of everyone, and sent back to al-Dhuhli what he had written from him carried by a camel-driver, for Muslim openly subscribed to the pronunciation and made no attempt to conceal it." . . . Ahmad ibn Mansur al-Shirazi also narrated it from Muhammad ibn Ya'qub, adding: "And Ahmad ibn Salama stood up and followed him."[151]

The Ash'ari view concerning the *maktūb* or content of writing is the same as al-Bukhari's, as shown by Bayhaqi's expression in *al-Asma' wa al-Sifat* (1:478, 2:125): "The *maktūb* is Allah's speech and one of His attributes inseparable from Him."

What possibly reconciles the different views on this subject is that *lafz* is used by some to mean the revealed, uncreated words and contents of recitation, while others mean thereby the mere act of pronunciation, which is created; hence the extreme caution shown by some, such as Imam al-Bukhari, who fell short of saying: "My *lafz* is created" even though he used it in the second sense, since he said: "*Lafz* is an act of human beings, and our acts are created." This lexical ambiguity is a proof of sorts that the differences on this particular question were largely in terminology rather than essence. Added to

---

[150]Nor the imam and hadith master of Khurasan: al-Husayn ibn Muhammad ibn Zyad, Abu 'Ali al-Naysaburi al-Qabbani (d. 289), whom al-Hakim described as "One of the pillars of hadith and hadith masters in the world." Dhahabi, *Siyar* (11:51-54).

[151]Al-Dhahabi, *Siyar* (10:314-315). Cf. Bayhaqi's *al-Asma' wa al-Sifat* (al-Hashidi ed. 2:20-21 #591).

this is a fundamental difference in method around the appropriateness of such dialectic, which poisoned the air with unnecessary condemnations on the part of Imam Ahmad's followers – and Allah knows best.

We did not detail this obsolete page of history except by way of explanation for al-Bayhaqi's and Ibn 'Abd al-Salam's texts, and to show that even the greatest scholars were liable to treat each other unfairly due to misunderstandings. In some of these questions it is obvious that many originally justifiable positions from Imam Ahmad took a life of their own to crystallize into extreme statements and even grave errors at the hands of his epigones. Those errors generally bear the stamp of literalism, and are being propagated in one form or another today by certain parties less knowledgeable than the scholars of the past by far. Their aberrant doctrines are detailed in other publications of Al-Sunna Foundation such as Shaykh Muhammad Hisham Kabbani's *Islamic Beliefs and Doctrine According to Ahl al-Sunna, The Doctrine of Ahl al-Sunna Versus the "Salafi" Movement,* and the *Encyclopedia of Islamic Doctrine.*[152]

---

[152]See also Shaykh 'Abd al-Fattah Abu Ghudda's monograph entitled *Mas'alat Khalq al-Qur'an wa Atharuha fi Sufuf al-Riwat wa al-Muhaddithin wa Kutub al-Jarh wa al-Ta'dil* ("The Question of the Createdness of the Qur'an and its Scathing Effect on the Ranks of the Narrators and Hadith Scholars As Well As on the Books of Narrator-Authentication").

Appendix 8

The Literalist Invalidation of Reason
(TA 'TÎL AL- 'AQL)

Al-'aql: "One of different types of necessary types of knowledge that characterize animate beings endowed with speech. Its seat is the heart."[153]

Al-'aql: "Lexically, 'the prevention' *(al-man')*, as it prevents its owner from straying from the correct path. Conventionally, it is an instinct *(gharîza)* through which one is prepared to comprehend the theoretical sciences. It is also said to be a light cast into the heart."[154]

Ahl al-Sunna charge literalists with the rejection of reason on the basis of exclusive resort to the patent meaning *(zâhir)* of transmitted evidence *(al-manqûl)*. The invalidation of reason was notably practiced by the *Khawârij*, the *Hashwiyya*, Ibn Hazm, and Ibn Taymiyya. After being consistently refuted by the scholars of the Four Sunni Schools it was revived by the Wahhabi movement two hundred years ago. This is shown by al-Zahawi (d. 1936CE) in *al-Fajr al-Sadiq* from which we quote the following excerpt (p. 36-44):

One of Ibn 'Abd al-Wahhab's more enormous stupidities is this: When he sees reason going against his claims, he casts aside all modesty and suspends reason giving it no role in his judgment. He endeavors thereby to make people like dumb beasts when it comes to matters of faith. He prohibits reason to enter into religious affairs despite the fact that there is no contradiction between reason and faith. On the contrary, whenever human minds reach their full measure of completeness and perfection, religion's merits and prerogatives with regard to reason become totally manifest. Is there in this age, an age of the mind's progress, anything more abominable than denying reason its proper scope, especially when the cardinal pivot of religion and the capacity to perform its duties is based on the ability to reason? For the obligation to carry out the duties of Islam falls away when mental capacity is absent. Allah has addressed his

---

[153]Ahmad ibn Hanbal in *Tabaqat al-Habanila* (2:281).
[154]Zakariyya al-Ansari, *al-Hudud al-Aniqa* (p. 67). Cf. n. 48 above.

servants in many places in the Qur'an: ⟨**O you who possess understanding**⟩ (cf. 65:10) alerting them to the fact that knowledge of the realities of religion is only a function of those possessed of minds. . . .

Since clear reason and sound theory clash in every way with what the Wahhabis believe, they are forced to cast reason aside. Thus by their taking the text of Qur'an and Sunna only in their apparent meaning *(zahir)* absurdity results. Indeed, this is the well-spring of their error and misguidance. For by attending only to the apparent meaning of the Qur'anic text, they believe that Allah being established over His throne and being high above His throne is literally true; that He literally has a face and two hands; that His coming down and His going up are a literal going down and coming up; that He may be pointed to in the sky with the fingers in a sensible manner, and so forth. According to this interpretation, Allah is made into nothing less than a body. These very Wahhabis, who call visiting graves idol-worship, become themselves idol-worshippers by fashioning the object they worship into a body, and treating it like an animal who sits on its seat and literally comes down and goes up and literally has a hand and a foot and fingers. But the true object of worship, Allah the Exalted, transcends what they worship.

Still, if one refutes them by rational proofs and establishes that their beliefs contradict the nature of divinity by criteria recognized by reason, they answer that there is no arena for humble human minds in matters like this, whose level is beyond the level of mere reason. In this respect they are exactly like Christians in their claim about the Trinity. Ask a Christian: "How is three one and one three?" They will answer: "Knowledge of the Trinity is above reason; it is impermissible to apply reasoning in this area."

There is no doubt that when reason and the transmitted text contradict each other, the transmitted text is interpreted by reason. For often it is impossible for a single judgment to affirm what each of them requires because of what is entailed by the simultaneous holding together of two contradictory propositions. Taking one side or the other, in other words, does not relieve the conflict. On the contrary, one must choose either priority of the transmitted text over

reason or reason over the transmitted text. Now the first of these two alternatives has to be invalid simply because it represents the invalidation of the root by the branch.

Clearly, one can affirm the transmitted text only by virtue of reason. That is because affirmation of the Creator, knowledge of prophecy and the rest of the conditions of a transmitted text's soundness are only fulfilled by aid of reason. Thus reason is the principle behind the transmitted text on which its soundness depends. So, if the transmitted text is given precedence over reason and its legal implication established by itself aside from the exercise of reason, then the root would be invalidated by the branch. And from that, the invalidation of the branch would follow as well. For the soundness of the transmitted text is derived from the judgment of reason, whose corruption is made possible when reason is invalidated.

Reason, then, is never cut off by the soundness of the transmitted text. Hence, it follows that declaring the transmitted text sound by making it prior to reason constitutes nothing less than the voiding of its soundness. But, if making something sound accomplishes its corruption, we face a contradiction: the transmitted text, then, is invalid. Therefore, if the priority of the transmitted text over reason does not exist on the basis of the preceding argument, then we have determined that reason has priority over the transmitted text. And that is what we set out to prove.

Once one realizes this, one also realizes without question the necessity of interpreting the Qur'anic verses where the apparent sense contradicts reason when the said verses are obscure and do not refer to things that are known with certainty *(yaqinât)*. On the one hand, there is general interpretation where the detailed clarification is left to Allah *(tafwid tafsilih)*. This is the school of the majority of the Pious Ancestors of our Faith *(al-Salaf)*. On the other hand, we have interpretation which sets out the text's meaning in keener fashion. The majority of later scholars *(al-khalaf)* follow the latter. In their view:

- The term "to firmly establish" as in the verse of Qur'an: 〈**The All-Merciful established Himself over the throne**〉 (20:4) means "He took possession of it" *(istawla)*. This is supported by the words of the poet who said: "'Amr took possession *(qad istawla)* of Iraq without bloodshed or sword."[155]

- Allah's saying: 〈**And your Lord shall arrive with angels rank on rank**〉 (89:22) means his power comes.[156]

- His saying: 〈**Unto Him the good word ascends**〉 (35:10) means: good words please Him. For the word is an accident [or sign] for which, by itself, locomotion is impossible.[157]

- His saying: 〈**Wait they for naught else than that Allah should come unto them in the shadows of the clouds with the angels?**〉 (2:210) means that His punishment should come unto them.[158]

- His saying: 〈**Then he drew near and came down until he was two bows' length or nearer**〉 (53:8-9) means the Prophet 🕌 came near Him by virtue of his obedience. The length of two bow-lengths is a pictorial representation in sensible fashion of what the mind understands.[159]

- In the Prophet's 🕌 saying in Bukhari and Muslim: "Allah comes down to the nearest heaven and says: who is repenting, I shall turn to him, and who seeks forgiveness, I shall forgive him" the

---

[155]Cf. al-Qurtubi's *Tafsir* (verses 2:29 and 7:54). See, for discussion of this meaning, the Appendix entitled "*Istiwa'* is a Divine Act" in our translation of al-Bayhaqi's *al-Asma' wa al-Sifat*, published separately.

[156]Al-Khallal in his book *al-Sunna*, reports that Imam Ahmad interpreted Sura al-Baqara figuratively to mean "Allah's reward" in the hadith of Muslim: "On the Day of the Rising, al-Baqara and Al 'Imran will come..."

[157]See Appendix, "Unto Him the Good Word Ascends."

[158]See the Appendix entitled , "Allah's 'Coming' and 'Arrival'" in our translation of al-Bayhaqi's *al-Asma' wa al-Sifat*, published separately.

[159]Ibn Hajar: "The scholars have solved its difficulty, as al-Qadi 'Iyad said in *al-Shifa'*: 'The attribution of drawing-near and proximity to Allah 🕌 does not pertain to place or time, but only to the Prophet 🕌 specifically, so as to reveal the magnificence of his rank and uttermost nobility. In relation to Allah, it consists in the bestowal of intimacy with His Prophet and His munificence towards him." *Fath al-Bari* (1959 ed. 13:487 #7079).

coming down signifies Allah's mercy.[160] He specifies night because it is the time of seclusion and various kinds of acts of humility and worship and so forth, as found in many verses of the Qur'an and narrations of the Prophet ﷺ.[161]

---

[160]As reported also from some of the Salaf, such as Imam Malik with a weak chain: see Ibn 'Abd al-Barr, *al-Tamhid* (7:143) and Dhahabi, *Siyar A'lam al-Nubala'* (8:105).

[161]Jamal Effendi Sidqi al-Zahawi, *al-Fajr al-Sadiq fi al-Radd 'ala Munkiri Karamat al-Awliya' wa al-Khawariq* ("The True Dawn: Refutation of Those Who Deny the Miracles of the Saints and the Suspension of Natural Laws"), translated and published as *The Doctrine of Ahl al-Sunna Versus the "Salafi" Movement* (Kazi Publications, USA, 1996) by Shaykh Muhammad Hisham Kabbani.

Appendix 9

"Unto Him The Good Word Ascends"

⟨Unto Him the good word ascends and the good deed raises it[162]⟩
(35:10).

Al-Tabari: "Al-Hasan and Qatada said: 'Allah does not accept *(la yaqbalu)* any word without deed; whoever speaks good words and does good deeds, Allah accepts it from him.'" Al-Qurtubi: "Ascent is upward movement which is inconceivable of words for they are accidents [or signs] *(a'rad)*. Ascent here stands for acceptance." The same is found in Abu Hayyan's *Tafsir al-Bahr al-Muhit*. Ibn Hajar: "Al-Farra' said: 'The meaning of the verse is that the good deed carries up the good word. That is, the latter is accepted if there is a good deed with it.' Al-Bayhaqi said: 'The ascent of the good word and the good charity stands for acceptance.'"[163] Al-Mahalli in *Tafsir al-Jalalayn*: "**Ascends**: i.e. He knows it; **He raises it**: i.e. He accepts it."

Ibn Jahbal said in his *Refutation of Ibn Taymiyya*:

42. ⟨Unto Him the good word ascends⟩ (35:10)... The sense of ascension here is none other than acceptance *(al-qabul)*, without inkling of boundary nor location.

The report that Imam Malik said: "Allah is in the heaven and His knowledge is in every place" is inauthentic as it is narrated through Ahmad ibn Hanbal from Shurayh ibn Na'man al-Hamdani al-Sa'idi al-Kufi from 'Abd Allah ibn Nafi' al-Sa'igh from Malik.[164] Shurayh's grading is "passable" *(salih)* and credible" *(saduq)* according to al-Dhahabi and Ibn Hajar respectively,[165] neither of which grading is enough to raise his narrations to the grade of "fair" *(hasan)* without confirmation from other narrations of equal or better strength for the same report. Accordingly the narrations which he alone transmits are weak. Further, Ahmad himself declared 'Abd Allah ibn

---

[162]Or: ⟨and the good deed He raises up.⟩
[163]In *Fath al-Bari* (1959 ed. 13:416).
[164]In al-Dhahabi's *Mukhtasar al-'Uluw* (p. 247) and al-Ajurri's *al-Shari'a* (p. 293 #663-664).
[165]In *Mizan al-I'tidal* (2:269 #3689) and *Taqrib al-Tahdhib* (p. 265 #2777).

Nafi' al-Sa'igh weak *(da'if)*, and al-Bukhari questioned his memorization, while Ibn 'Adi stated that he transmitted oddities *(ghara'ib)* from Malik.[166] The narration is further weakened by the fact that Shurayh is "virtually unknown" as stated by Abu Hatim al-Razi;[167] nor is he known to narrate from 'Abd Allah ibn Nafi' but from 'Ali ibn Abi Talib; nor is Imam Ahmad recorded as narrating from him.

As for the content of the above report, it is made dubious by the fact that Malik was well-known to condemn any statements about Allah's Entity and Attributes other than sound reports,[168] particularly statements that suggest anthropomorphism,[169] ordering that the verses and hadiths of the attributes be passed on exactly as they came,[170] and even forbidding that hadiths such as "Allah created Adam in his/His image" be narrated lest people be confused by them.[171] Malik's strong affirmation of transcendence *(tanzih)* is also famous, as illustrated by his characterization of *istiwa'* as inconceivable[172] – thus precluding any anthropomorphic notions[173] – and his verdict against

---

[166]Al-Dhahabi, *Mizan* (2:513-514 #4647); Ibn 'Adi, *al-Kamil* (4:242 #1070). Dr. Nur al-Din 'Itr, however, points out in his margins on al-Dhahabi's *al-Mughni fi al-Du'afa'* (1:513 #3396) that al-Sa'igh is very reliable when narrating from Malik.

[167]In al-Dhahabi's *al-Mughni fi al-Du'afa'* (1:425 #2759).

[168]Al-Shatibi stated in *al-Muwafaqat* (2:332): "Malik ibn Anas used to say: 'I detest talking about Religion, just as the people of our country [al-Madina] detest and prohibit it, in the sense of Jahm's doctrine, *qadar*, and the like. I do not like to speak except about what relates to practice.'"

[169]For example, Malik said: "Allah is neither ascribed a limit nor likened with anything" *(la yuhaddad wa la yushabbah)*. Ibn al-'Arabi, *Ahkam al-Qur'an* (4:1740).

[170]As mentioned by al-Tirmidhi in his *Sunan* (Book of *zakat*, hadith "Verily, Allah accepts the *zakat* and takes it with His right Hand..."), Ibn al-Jawzi in his *Daf' Shubah al-Tashbih* (p. 195-196), al-Dhahabi in *Siyar A'lam al-Nubala'* (al-Arna'ut ed. 8:105), Ibn Abi Zayd al-Qayrawani, *al-Jami'* (p. 124), and others.

[171]Al-'Uqayli, *al-Du'afa'* (2:251 #806). Cf. Dhahabi, *Mizan al-I'tidal* (3:645 #7938).

[172]Narrated from Yahya ibn Yahya al-Tamimi, Rabi'a ibn Abi 'Abd al-Rahman, and Ja'far ibn 'Abd Allah by al-Bayhaqi with a sound chain in *al-Asma' wa al-Sifat* (2:305-306 #867), Ibn Abi Zayd al-Qayrawani in *al-Jami' fi al-Sunan* (p. 123), and al-Dhahabi in the *Siyar* (7:415). Note that the wording that says: "The 'how' is unknown" *(al-kayfu majhul)* is falsely attributed to Imam Malik, although also cited from Rabi'a with a sound chain by al-Bayhaqi in *al-Asma' wa al-Sifat* (2:306 #868) and without chain by Ibn al-'Arabi in *'Arida al-Ahwadhi* (2:235), but is an aberrant narration *(riwaya shadhdha)*. Yet it is the preferred wording of Ibn Taymiyya in *Dar' Ta'arud al-'Aql wa al-Naql* (1:278) and *Majmu'a al-Fatawa* (17:373) as he infers from it support for his positions.

[173]As stated by Shaykh al-Islam Taqi al-Din al-Subki in *al-Sayf al-Saqil* (p. 128).

anyone that points to his own hand or eye while referring to the corresponding divine Attributes.[174]

---

[174]Ibn Wahb reported: "I heard Malik [ibn Anas] say: 'Whoever recites ❴**Allah's Hand**❵ (3:73, 5:64, 48:10, 57:29) and indicates his hand, or recites ❴**Allah's Eye**❵ (cf. 20:39, 11:37, 23:27, 52:48, 54:14) and indicates that organ of his: let it be cut off to discipline him over Allah's sacredness and transcendence above what he has compared Him to, and above his own comparison to Him.'" In Ibn al-'Arabi, *Ahkam al-Qur'an* (4:1740).

Bibliography

'Abd al-Khaliq, 'Abd al-Ghani. *Hujjiyya al-Sunna.* Herndon, VA: Dar al-Wafa', 1993.

'Abd al-Qahir al-Baghdadi. *Usul al-Din.* Istanbul: Dar al-Funun fi Madrasa al-Ilahiyyat, 1928.

-------. *al-Farq Bayn al-Firaq.* Beirut: Dar al-Kutub al-'Ilmiyya, n.d.

Abu Dawud. *Sunan.* 3 vols. Ed. Muhammad Fouad 'Abd al-Baqi. Beirut: Dar al-Kutub al-'Ilmiyya, 1996.

Abu Dawud al-Tayalisi, see al-Tayalisi.

Abu Hanifa. *Al-Fiqh al-Akbar.* See al-Qari, *Sharh al-Fiqh al-Akbar.*

-------. *Wasiyya al-Imam al-A'zam Abu Hanifa.* Ed. Fu'ad 'Ali Rida. Beirut: Maktabat al-Jamahir, 1970.

Abu Ya'la al-Musili. *Musnad.* 13 vols. Ed. Husayn Salim Asad. Damascus: Dar al-Ma'mun li al-Turath, 1984.

Abu Nu'aym al-Asfahani. *Hilya al-Awliya' wa Tabaqat al-Asfiya'.* 12 vols. Ed. Mustafa 'Abd al-Qadir 'Ata. Beirut: Dar al-Kutub al-'Ilmiyya, 1997.

Abu Zahra. *Abu Hanifa: Hayatuhu wa 'Asruhu, Ara'uhu wa Fiqhuh.* Cairo: Dar al-Fikr al-'Arabi, 1997. [Repr. of the 1947 ed. with bibl. revisions.]

Al-Ahdab, Khaldun. *Zawa'id Tarikh Baghdad 'Ala al-Kutub al-Sitta.* 10 vols. Damascus: Dar al-Qalam, 1996.

Ahmad ibn Hanbal. *Al-Musnad.* 20 vols. Ed. Ahmad Shakir and Hamza Ahmad al-Zayn. Cairo: Dar al-Hadith, 1995.

Al-'Ajluni. *Kashf al-Khafa.* 2nd ed. 2 vols. Beirut: Dar Ihya' al-Turath al-'Arabi, 1932.

Al-Ajurri. *Al-Shari'a.* Ed. 'Abd al-Razzaq al-Mahdi. Beirut: Dar al-Kitab al-'Arabi, 1996.

Al-Ansari, Zakariyya. *Al-Hudud al-Aniqa wa al-Ta'rifat al-Daqiqa.* Beirut: Dar al-Fikr al-Mu'asir, 1991.

Al-Ash'ari, Abu al-Hasan. *Al-Ibana 'an Usul al-Diyana.* Ed. Fawqiyya H. Mahmud. Cairo: Dar al-Ansar, 1977.

-------. *Al-Ibana 'an Usul al-Diyana.* Ed. 'Abbas Sabbagh. Beirut: Dar al-Nafa'is, 1994.

-------. *Al-Ibana 'an Usul al-Diyana.* Ed. Bashir Muhammad 'Uyun. Damascus and Beirut: Dar al-Bayan, 1996.

Al-'Azim Abadi, Muhammad Shams al-Haqq. *'Awn al-Ma'bud Sharh Sunan Abi Dawud.* 14 vols. in 7. Beirut: Dar al-Kutub al-'Ilmiyya, n.d. Includes Abu Dawud's *Sunan.*

Al-Bajuri. *Hashiya 'ala Matn al-Sanusiyya fi al-'Aqida.* Ed. 'Abd al-Salam Shannar. Damascus: Dar al-Bayruti, 1994.

Al-Bayhaqi. *Al-Asma' wa al-Sifat.* Ed. Muhammad Zahid al-Kawthari. Beirut: Dar Ihya' al-Turath al-'Arabi, n.d. Reprint of the 1358/1939 Cairo edition.

-------. *Al-Asma' wa al-Sifat.* 2 vols. Ed. 'Abd Allah al-Hashidi. Riyad: Maktaba al-Sawadi, 1993.

-------. *Al-Madkhal ila al-Sunan al-Kubra.* Ed. Muhammad Diya' al-Rahman al-A'zami. Al-Kuwait: Dar al-Khulafa' li al-Kitab al-Islami, n.d.

-------. *Manaqib al-Shafi'i.* 2 vols. Ed. Ahmad Saqr. Cairo: Dar al-Turath, n. d.

-------. *Al-Sunan al-Kubra.* 10 vols. Ed. Muhammad 'Abd al-Qadir 'Ata. Mecca: Maktaba Dar al-Baz, 1994.

Al-Bukhari. *Khalq Af'al al-'Ibad.* Beirut: Mu'assasa al-Risala, 1990.

-------. *Sahih.* Ed. Ahmad 'Ali al-Siharanfuri. 1272/1856.

-------. *Sahih.* 8 vols. in 3. Ed. Muhammad al-Zuhri al-Ghamrawi. Bulaq: al-Matba'a al-Kubra al-Amiriyya, 1314/1896. Reprint, Cairo: Mustafa Baba al-Halabi, 1323/1905.

-------. *Sahih.* See Ibn Hajar, *Fath al-Bari.*

Al-Buti. *Kubra al-Yaqinat al-Kawniyya.* Beirut and Damascus: Dar al-Fikr, 1997.

-------. *Al-Salafiyya Marhalatun Zamaniyyatun Mubaraka La Madhhabun Islami.* Damascus: Dar al-Fikr, 1988.

Al-Dhahabi, Muhammad Shams al-Din. *Mizan al-I'tidal.* 4 vols. Ed. 'Ali Muhammad al-Bajawi. Beirut: Dar al-Ma'rifa, 1963.

-------. *Al-Mughni fi al-Du'afa'.* 2 vols. Ed. Nur al-Din 'Itr. Qatar: Idara Ihya' al-Turath al-Islami, 1987.

-------. *Mukhtasar al-'Uluw li al-'Ali al-Ghaffar.* Ed. M. Nasir al-Din al-Albani. Beirut: al-Maktab al-Islami, 1991[2].

-------. *Siyar A'lam al-Nubala'.* 19 vols. Ed. Muhibb al-Din al-'Amrawi. Beirut: Dar al-Fikr, 1996.

-------. *Tadhkira al-Huffaz.* 4 vols. in 2. Ed. 'Abd al-Rahman ibn Yahya al-Mu'allimi. A fifth volume, titled *Dhayl Tadhkira al-Huffaz*, consists in al-Husayni's *Dhayl Tadhkira al-Huffaz*, Muhammad ibn Fahd al-Makki's *Lahz al-Alhaz bi Dhayl Tadhkira al-Huffaz*, and al-Suyuti's *Dhayl Tabaqat al-Huffaz*. Ed. Muhammad Zahid al-Kawthari. Beirut: Dar Ihya' al-Turath al-'Arabi and Dar al-Kutub al-'Ilmiyya, n.d. Reprint of the 1968 Hyderabad edition.

Al-Fattani. *Tadhkira al-Mawdu'at.* Cairo: al-Matba'a al-Muniriyya, 1343/1924-1925.

Al-Hakim. *Al-Mustadrak 'Ala al-Sahihayn.* With al-Dhahabi's *Talkhis al-Mustadrak.* 5 vols. Indexes by Yusuf 'Abd al-Rahman al-Mar'ashli. Beirut: Dar al-Ma'rifa, 1986.

-------. *Al-Mustadrak 'Ala al-Sahihayn.* With al-Dhahabi's *Talkhis al-Mustadrak.* 4 vols. Annotations by Mustafa 'Abd al-Qadir 'Ata'. Beirut: Dar al-Kutub al-'Ilmiyya, 1990.

Al-Haytami, Ahmad. *Al-Fatawa al-Hadithiyya.* Cairo: Mustafa al-Baba al-Halabi, Repr. 1989.

Al-Haythami, Nur al-Din. *Majma' al-Zawa'id wa Manba' al-Fawa'id.* 3rd ed. 10 vols. Beirut: Dar al-Kitab al-'Arabi, 1982.

Ibn 'Abd al-Barr. *Jami' Bayan al-'Ilm wa Fadlih.* 2 vols. Ed. Abu al-Ashbal al-Zuhayri. Dammam: Dar Ibn al-Jawzi, 1994.

Ibn 'Abd al-Salam. *Fatawa.* Ed. 'Abd al-Rahman ibn 'Abd al-Fattah. Beirut: Dar al-Ma'rifa, 1986.

-------. *Al-Ishara ila al-Ijaz fi Ba'd Anwa' al-Majaz.* Ed. 'Uthman Hilmi. <Bulaq?> Al-Matba'a al-'Amira, 1313/1895.

-------. *Ma'na al-Iman wa al-Islam aw al-Farq Bayn al-Iman wa al-Islam.* Ed. Iyad Khalid al-Tabba'. Beirut and Damascus: Dar al-Fikr, 1995[2].

-------. *Al-Mulha fi I'tiqad Ahl al-Haqq.* In *Rasa'il al-Tawhid.* Ed. Iyad Khalid al-Tabba'. Beirut and Damascus: Dar al-Fikr, 1995. Also in Ibn al-Subki, *Tabaqat al-Shafi'iyya al-Kubra,* vol. 8 p. 219-229.

-------. *Qawa'id al-Ahkam fi Masalih al-Anam.* 2 vols. Dar al-Sharq li al-Tiba'a, 1388/1968.

Ibn Abi Ya'la. *Tabaqat al-Hanabila.* 2 vols. Ed. Muhammad Hamid al-Fiqqi. Cairo: Dar Ihya' al-Kutub al-'Arabiyya, n.d.

Ibn Abi Zayd al-Qayrawani. *Al-Jami' fi al-Sunan wa al-Adab wa al-Maghazi wa al-Tarikh.* Ed. M. Abu al-Ajfan and 'Uthman Battikh. Beirut: Mu'assasa al-Risala; Tunis: al-Maktaba al-'Atiqa, 1982.

Ibn 'Adi. *Al-Kamil fi Du'afa' al-Rijal.* 7 vols. Ed. Yahya Mukhtar Ghazawi. Beirut: Dar al-Fikr, 1988.

Ibn 'Asakir. *Tabyin Kadhib al-Muftari Fi Ma Nasaba ila al-Imam Abi al-Hasan al-Ash'ari.* Ed. Ahmad Hijazi al-Saqqa. Beirut: Dar al-Jil, 1995.

Ibn 'Ata' Allah. *Al-Hikam.* Ed. and trans. Paul Nwiya. In *Ibn 'Ata' Allah et la naissance de la confrerie shadhilite.* Beirut: Dar al-Machreq, 1990.[2]

Ibn al-Athir. *Al-Nihaya fi Gharib al-Athar.* 5 vols. Eds. Tahir Ahmad al-Zawi and Mahmud Muhammad al-Tabbakhi. Beirut: Dar al-Fikr, 1979.

Ibn Hajar. *Fath al-Bari Sharh Sahih al-Bukhari.* 14 vols. Notes by 'Abd al-'Aziz ibn Baz. Beirut: Dar al-Kutub al-'Ilmiyya, 1989. Includes al-Bukhari's *Sahih.*

-------. *Ibidem.* 13 vols. Ed. Muhammad Fouad 'Abd al-Baqi and Muhibb al-Din al-Khatib. Beirut: Dar al-Ma'rifa, 1959.

-------. *Lisan al-Mizan.* 7 vols. Hyderabad: Da'ira al-Ma'arif al-Nizamiyya, 1329/1911. Repr. Beirut: Mu'assassa al-A'lami, 1986.

-------. *Tahdhib al-Tahdhib.* 14 vols. Hyderabad: Da'ira al-Ma'arif al-Nizamiyya, 1327/1909. Repr. Beirut: Dar al-Fikr, 1984.

-------. *Taqrib al-Tahdhib.* Ed. Muhammad 'Awwama. Aleppo: Dar al-Rashid, 1997.

-------. *Tawali al-Ta'sis li Ma'ali Muhammad ibn Idris.* Ed. 'Abd Allah al-Qadi. Beirut: Dar al-Kutub al-'Ilmiyya, 1986.

Ibn Hibban. *Sahih Ibn Hibban bi Tartib Ibn Balban.* 18 vols. Ed. Shu'ayb al-Arna'ut. Beirut: Mu'assasa al-Risala, 1993.

Ibn 'Imad. *Shadharat al-Dhahab fi Akhbar Man Dhahab.* 8 vols. Beirut: Dar Ihya' al-Turath al-'Arabi, n.d.

Ibn al-Jawzi. *Daf' Shubah al-Tashbih bi Akuff al-Tanzih.* Ed. Hasan 'Ali al-Saqqaf. Amman: Dar al-Imam Nawawi, 1991. Ed. al-Kawthari. Repr. Cairo: al-Maktaba al-Azhariyya li al-Turath, 1998.

-------. *Al-'Ilal al-Mutanahiya fi al-Ahadith al-Wahiya.* 2 vols. Ed. Shaykh Khalil al-Mays. Beirut: Dar al-Kutub al-'Ilmiyya, 1983.

-------. *Manaqib al-Imam Ahmad.* 2nd ed. Ed. Muhammad Amin al-Khanji al-Kutbi. Beirut: Khanji wa Hamdan, 1349/1930-1931.

Ibn Kathir. *Al-Bidaya wa al-Nihaya.* 15 vols. Ed. Editing Board of al-Turath. Beirut: Dar Ihya' al-Turath al-'Arabi, 1993.

Ibn Majah. *Sunan.* See al-Suyuti *et al., Sharh Sunan Ibn Majah.*

Ibn Qudama, Muwaffaq al-Din. *Lam'a al-I'tiqad.* Ed. 'Abd al-Qadir Badran and Bashir Muhammad 'Uyun. Damascus: Dar al-Bayan, 1992.

Ibn Qutayba. *Ta'wil Mukhtalaf al-Hadith.* Ed. Muhammad Zuhri al-Najjar. Beirut: Dar al-Jil, 1972.

-------. *Ta'wil Mukhtalaf al-Hadith.* Ed. Muhammad 'Abd al-Rahim. Beirut: Dar al-Fikr, 1995.

Ibn Rajab. *Jami' al-'Ulum wa al-Hikam.* 2 vols. Ed. Wahba al-Zuhayli. Beirut: Dar al-Khayr, 1996.

Ibn Sallam. *Gharib al-Hadith.* 2 vols. Beirut: Dar al-Kitab al-'Arabi, 1976; Dar al-Kutub al-'Ilmiyya, 1986. Neither edition mentions the editor.

Ibn al-Subki, Taj al-Din. *Qa'ida fi al-Jarh wa al-Ta'dil.* Ed. 'Abd al-Fattah Abu Ghudda. 2nd ed. Cairo, 1978. 5th ed. Aleppo & Beirut: Maktab al-Matbu'at al-Islamiyya, 1984.

-------. *Tabaqat al-Shafi'iyya al-Kubra.* 10 vols. Ed. Mahmud M. al-Tannahi and 'Abd al-Fattah M. al-Hilw. 2nd. ed. Jiza: Dar Hijr, 1992.

Ibn Taymiyya. *Dar' Ta'arud al-'Aql wa al-Naql* [= *Muwafaqa al-Ma'qul wa al-Manqul*]. Ed. Muhammad al-Sayyid Julaynid. Cairo: Mu'assasa al-Ahram, 1988.

Al-'Iraqi. *Tarh al-Tathrib fi Sharh al-Taqrib.* 8 vols. in 4. Ed. Mahmud Hasan Rabi'. Beirut: Dar Ihya' al-Turath al-'Arabi, 1992. Repr. of the Cairo edition.

Kabbani, Shaykh Muhammad Hisham. *The Doctrine of Ahl al-Sunna Versus the "Salafi" Movement.* Mountain View: Al-Sunna Foundation of America, 1996.

-------. *Encyclopedia of Islamic Doctrine.* 7 vols. Moutain View: Al-Sunna Foundation of America, 1998.

-------. *Islamic Beliefs and Doctrine According to Ahl al-Sunna.* Vol. 1. Mountain View: Al-Sunna Foundation of America, 1996.

Al-Kattani, al-Sayyid Muhammad ibn Ja'far. *Nazm al-Mutanathir fi al-Hadith al-Mutawatir.* Beirut: Dar al-Kutub al-'Ilmiyya, 1980.

Keller, Noah Ha Mim, ed. and trans. *The Reliance of the Traveller.* Dubai: Modern Printing Press, 1991. Translation of Ahmad ibn Naqib al-Misri's *'Umda al-Salik.*

Al-Khatib al-Baghdadi. *Tarikh Baghdad.* 14 vols. Madina: al-Maktaba al-Salafiyya, n.d. See also al-Ahdab, *Zawa'id Tarikh Baghdad.*

Lahmar, Hamid. *Al-Imam Malik Mufassiran.* Beirut: Dar al-Fikr, 1995.

Malik. *Al-Muwatta'.* 2 vols. Ed. Muhammad Fouad 'Abd al-Baqi. Beirut: Dar al-Kutub al-'Ilmiyya, n.d.

Al-Mizzi. *Tahdhib al-Kamal.* 35 vols. Ed. Bashshar 'Awwad Ma'ruf. Beirut: Mu'assasa al-Risala, 1980.

Al-Mubarakfuri. *Tuhfa al-Ahwadhi bi Sharh Jami' al-Tirmidhi.* 10 vols. Beirut: Dar al-Kutub al-'Ilmiyya, 1990. Includes al-Tirmidhi's *Sunan.*

Al Munawi. *Fayd al-Qadir.* 2nd ed. 6 vols. Beirut: Dar al Ma'rifa, 1972.

Muslim. *Sahih.* 5 vols. Ed. M. Fuad 'Abd al-Baqi. Beirut: Dar Ihya' al-Turath al-'Arabi, 1954. Also see al-Nawawi, *Sharh Sahih Muslim.*

Al-Nasa'i. *Sunan.* See al-Suyuti, *Sharh Sunan al-Nasa'i.*

Al-Nawawi. *Sharh Sahih Muslim.* 18 vols. Ed. Khalil al-Mays. Beirut: Dar al-Kutub al-'Ilmiyya, n.d. Includes Muslim's *Sahih.*

-------. *Tahdhib al-Asma' wa al-Lughat.* Cairo: Idara al-Tiba'a al-Muniriyya, [1927?].

Al-Qari. *Al-Asrar al-Marfu'a fi al-Ahadith al-Mawdu'a. (Al-Mawdu'at al-Kubra).* 2nd ed. Ed. Muhammad ibn Lutfi al-Sabbagh. Beirut and Damascus: al-Maktab al-Islami, 1986. [1st ed. 1971.]

-------. *Mirqat al-Mafatih Sharh Mishkat al-Masabih.* Together with Ibn Hajar's *Ajwiba 'Ala Risala al-Qazwini Hawla Ba'd Ahadith al-Masabih.* 11 vols. Ed. Sidqi Muhammad Jamil al-'Attar. Damascus: Dar al-Fikr, 1994.

Al-Quda'i. *Musnad al-Shihab.* 2 vols. Ed. Hamdi ibn 'Abd al-Majid al-Salafi. Beirut: Mu'assasa al-Risala, 1986.

Al-Qurtubi. *Al-Jami' li Ahkam al-Qur'an.* 2nd ed. 14 vols. Beirut: Dar Ihya' al-Turath al-'Arabi, 1952. Reprint.

Al-Qushayri. *Al-Risala.* Dar al-Tiba'a al-'Amira, 1287/1870.

-------. *Al-Rasa'il al-Qushayriyya.* Ed. Pir Muhammad Hasan. Sidon and Beirut: al-Maktaba al-'Asriyya, 1970.

Al-Razi, Muhammad ibn Abi Bakr. *Mukhtar al-Sihah.* Ed. Mahmud Khatir. Beirut: Maktaba Lubnan, 1995.

Al-Sakhawi, Muhammad ibn 'Abd al-Rahman. *Al-Jawahir wa al-Durar fi Manaqib Shaykh al-Islam Ibn Hajar.* Ed. Hamid Abd al-Majid and Taha al-Zayni. Cairo: Lajna Ihya' al-Turath al-Islami, 1986.

-------. *Al-Maqasid al-Hasana.* Ed. Muhammad 'Uthman al-Khisht. Beirut: Dar al-Kitab al-'Arabi, 1985.

Al-Saqqaf, Hasan 'Ali. *I'lam al-Kha'id bi Tahrim al-Qur'an 'ala al-Junub wa al-Ha'id.* Amman: Dar al-Imam al-Nawawi.

Shatta, Ibrahim al-Dusuqi. *Sira al-Shaykh al-Kabir Abi 'Abd Allah Muhammad ibn Khafif al-Shirazi.* Cairo: al-Hay'a al-'Amma li Shu'un al-Matabi' al-Amiriyya, 1977.

Al-Subki, Taj al-Din. See Ibn al-Subki.

Al-Subki, Taqi al-Din. *Al-Rasa'il al-Subkiyya fi al-Radd 'ala Ibn Taymiyya wa Tilmidhihi Ibn Qayyim al-Jawziyya.* Ed. Kamal al-Hut. Beirut: 'Alam al-Kutub, 1983.

-------. *Al-Sayf al-Saqil fi al-Radd 'ala Ibn Zafil*. Ed. al-Kawthari. Cairo: Matba'a al-Sa'ada, 1937.

Al-Suyuti. *Al-Dibaj 'ala Sahih Muslim ibn al-Hajjaj*. 6 vols. Ed. Abu Ishaq al-Juwayni al-Athari. Al-Khubar: Dar Ibn 'Affan, 1996.

-------. *Al-Durar al-Muntathira fi al-Ahadith al-Mushtahara*. Ed. Muhammad 'Abd al-Rahim. Beirut: Dar al-Fikr, 1995.

-------. *Sharh Sunan al-Nasa'i*. 9 vols. Ed. 'Abd al-Fattah Abu Ghudda. Aleppo & Beirut: Maktab al-Matbu'at al-Islamiyya, 1986. Includes al-Nasa'is' *Sunan*.

-------, 'Abd al-Ghani al-Dihlawi, and Fakhr al-Hasan al-Gangohi. *Sharh Sunan Ibn Majah*. Karachi: Qadimi Kutub Khana, n.d. Includes Ibn Majah's *Sunan*.

Al-Tabarani. *Al-Mu'jam al-Awsat*. 2 vols. Ed. Mahmud al-Tahhan. Riyadh: Maktaba al-Ma'arif, 1985.

-------. *Al-Mu'jam al-Kabir*. 20 vols. Ed. Hamdi ibn 'Abd al-Majid al-Salafi. Mosul: Maktaba al-'Ulum wa al-Hikam, 1983.

-------. *Al-Mu'jam al-Saghir*. 2 vols. Ed. Muhammad Shakur Mahmud. Beirut and Amman: Al-Maktab al-Islami, Dar 'Ammar, 1985.

Al-Tabari, Muhibb al-Din. *Al-Riyad al-Nadira*. 2 vols. Ed. 'Isa al-Humayri. Beirut: Dar al-Gharb al-Islami, 1996.

Al-Tahawi. *Mushkil al-Athar*. Hyderabad: Da'ira al-Ma'arif al-'Uthmaniyya, 1915.

Al-Tayalisi. *Musnad*. Beirut: Dar al-Kitab al-Lubnani; Dar al-Ma'rifa; Dar al-Tawfiq, n.d. All three are reprints of the 1321/1903 edition of Da'ira al-Ma'arif al-'Uthmaniyya in Hyderabad.

Al-Tirmidhi. *Sunan*. See al-Mubarakfuri, *Tuhfa al-Ahwadhi*.

Al-'Uqayli, *al-Du'afa' min al-Ruwat*. 4 vols. Ed. 'Abd al-Mu'it Amin Qal'aji. Beirut: Dar al-Kutub al-'Ilmiyya, 1984.

Al-Zarkashi. *Al-Tadhkira fi al-Ahadith al-Mushtahara*. Ed. Mustafa 'Abd al-Qadir 'Ata. Beirut: Dar al-Kutub al-'Ilmiyya, 1986.